THE PRINCIPLES AND METHODS OF
MUSICAL CRITICISM
By M. D. CALVOCORESSI

OXFORD UNIVERSITY PRESS
LONDON: HUMPHREY MILFORD
1923

Oxford University Press

London   Edinburgh   Glasgow   Copenhagen
New York   Toronto   Melbourne   Cape Town
Bombay   Calcutta   Madras   Shanghai
Humphrey Milford Publisher to the UNIVERSITY

PRINTED IN ENGLAND
AT THE OXFORD UNIVERSITY PRESS
BY FREDERICK HALL

TO ETHEL

IN DEEP GRATITUDE FOR HER CONSTANT

ENCOURAGEMENT AND HELP

PREFACE

It is the fate of all critics to have to confront a bewildering diversity of problems, some of which bear upon their artistic creeds, others upon their methods of work, and others upon the materials they work on.

These problems—and this is good—may counteract the aloofness and self-satisfaction inherent in the rule-of-thumb methods which might be, and often are, followed by critics who ignore them. But no matter how earnestly other critics seek enlightenment, much remains obscure, or at best open to challenge. The more conscientious the critic, the more often he will realize the doubtfulness of his conclusions.

The difficulties are greater for the critic of music than for other critics, because we know less of music than of any other art, and because although musical criticism is as ancient as all others, it lagged behind while the others were progressing. It is only of late that it began to show signs of method; and its particular problems are hardly realized yet. The critics to whose exertions it owes whatever headway it has made did not find in the writings of their predecessors the kind of help which the works of Goethe, Hegel, Sainte-Beuve, Taine, Matthew Arnold,

5

Poe, Wordsworth, Coleridge, Hazlitt, and others afford to literary and art critics of the present period.

This book is intended, primarily, for the student, but does not aim at solving his problems for him. Indeed, the ideal course would have been to determine these, the choice of available solutions, the methods through which the choice may be effected, and to leave the rest to him. It will be seen, however, that this ideal method is not rigorously followed here, the reason being that often no further progress would be made without a certain solution being admitted; and where no solution could be proved valid, nothing remained but to ask the reader to take one for granted.

This I steadfastly believe constantly occurs in art criticism, whichever the topic and method. One advantage of method is that it may help to determine when and where it occurs, and perhaps at times why.

The chief lesson which the student should learn is how to say exactly what he wishes to say—neither less nor more—and never to ask his readers to accept any statement except with open eyes.

We only understand a critic's point of view when we know what his tenets are. How both the writers of criticism and their readers may acquire this knowledge is what this book attempts to show. For this reason, I hope that it may prove useful not only to would-be critics, but to that portion of the music-loving public which reads criticisms and is interested enough in music, if not in criticism, to wish to know how judgements are formed; and that it

6

may show how conflicts between judgements may be accounted for.

Analysis and comparison of judgements on works, on composers, and on general problems of aesthetics constituted the main part of the lessons in the theory and practice of criticism delivered by me from 1909 to 1914 at the Paris École des Hautes Études Sociales, to which this book owes its inception. For the sole reason that it is with ideas in the abstract, and not with their authors or upholders that the analyst is concerned—exactly as the critic should be—some of the judgements adduced as examples here are given without information regarding their source.

Except in the last chapter, no reference is made to criticism of interpretation, which plays so great a part in the practising critic's everyday work of journalism. I may confess that even if I had wished to say more, I should have found myself unable to do so. The capacity to judge interpretation depends chiefly upon the sensitiveness and general musical education which it must be assumed that the critic possesses at the outset and is constantly increasing.

A perusal of this book will show that, in its author's opinion, the musical critic's studies should include a good deal besides all that properly refers to music as an art : various branches of philosophy, viz. psychology, aesthetics, and logic ; acoustics and other branches of musical science, if only in order to test the conclusions or assertions of writers who draw upon these for controversial purposes ; and history (not of music only), more on account of the mistakes which ignorance will occasion than for the help history affords in criticism proper. Experience in other arts and other modes of thought will prove the sole remedy against the dangers of specialization, which tends to narrow and warp the critic's outlook.

This, it will perhaps be said, is a good deal indeed for a man engaged in work which is often described as superfluous, or futile, or inferior, or detestable ; which some people hold (not altogether without excuse) as the last resource of those who fail in all other branches of music, writing, or reporting.

Yet, if we remember that to many of us music is an art which means more than anything else within the province of imagination ; if it be true that music is the most wonderful of arts as well as the most mysterious—an art to whose condition, Walter Pater has said, all other arts are constantly aspiring—and an art informed with the deepest significance for all to realize even if none can explain it : shall we, then, wonder that in order to deal at all with its problems, as much general and special information and labour should be required as is expected, as a matter of course, from anybody dealing with the other great provinces of imagination, thought, or experience?

The programme is ambitious. I hope I have succeeded at least in outlining it, even at the cost of finding it unavoidable to lay more than one rod in pickle for myself. In various quarters I have found help which I gratefully acknowledge. To John Lane,

8

The Bodley Head, Ltd., I am indebted for permission to reprint the extracts of J. M. Robertson's invaluable *New Essays towards a Critical Method*—a book which, as well as his older Essays, gave me more food for thought than any other. Clive Bell's *Since Cézanne* and *What is Art?* have been of great use to me, as I know the quotations from them I give will be to all readers. Among writings on music, none have proved more useful than Sir Henry Hadow's. This volume, in its course, will testify more fully than I could do in this Preface to my indebtedness to many other writers on music and other topics; so I shall content myself with paying tribute here to Charles Mill Gayley and Fred Newton Scott, whose admirable *Introduction to the Methods and Materials of Literary Criticism* has enabled me considerably to restrict the bulk of my present contribution.

To the *Musical Quarterly*, *Musical Times*, and *Monthly Musical Record* I am indebted for permission to reprint portions of my published articles; to my wife, for much time devoted to reading the manuscript and proofs of this volume. Older is my debt, which I gladly and thankfully acknowledge, to Monsieur André Lalande, once my master of Philosophy in Paris. If I have succeeded at all in my endeavours, it is chiefly to his teaching that my thanks should go.

M. D. CALVOCORESSI

Chelsea, *May* 1923

CONTENTS

PART I. THE THEORY

PART II. THE PRACTICE

PART I

THE THEORY

CHAPTER I

PRELIMINARY INVESTIGATION.
THE PROBLEMS STATED

I

THERE can hardly be a music-lover who has not encountered, in the course of his reading, some disparagement of works which are dear to him, or found praise bestowed upon works which he cordially dislikes or—still worse—considers hopelessly dull. And possibly these unpalatable and incomprehensible verdicts will emanate from the very critics whom he considers the most trustworthy and the most enlightened.

If he is in the habit of reading even a moderate amount of writings on music, he will hardly be surprised by judgements which not only differ, but are contradictory. But sooner or later, unless he inclines to pooh-pooh the whole matter, considering that it merely illustrates the impotence or the vanity of criticism (in which case he need read this book no further), he will wonder how such discrepancies can exist, and whether it is possible to unravel the tangle ; he will ask himself why the judgements which clash with his own, or with one another, have been uttered.

This is precisely what the critic at work should be constantly asking himself. The tendency of the untrained critic is either to rush in where it might be advisable to tread warily, or to remain unable to make up his mind. At first sight the prospect for the tiro who would learn to avoid either extreme is not particularly encouraging.

To say that hardly two writers tackle the appraisement or mere description of a work or of a composer's aims and achievements in the same spirit or according to the same methods is no exaggeration. The fact may now and then be disguised by the sameness of the arguments adduced and of the very vocabulary used; but this merely renders the confusion worse. If the position was simply that similar conclusions are reached by different methods or by methods founded on different principles, the harm would be small; but what we often see is that similar principles and methods lead to widely different conclusions.

The beginner who, realizing this condition of things, thinks it worth his while carefully to consider which course of procedure he is to adopt will stand in need of help. To the others help is even more needful, if only in the shape of a preliminary warning.

To investigate the causes and consequences of the discrepancies which the study of criticism in operation reveals, and to devise, in accordance with the results of the investigation, some comparatively safe course of procedure, is in itself criticism, and criticism of the very highest and most difficult order. It cannot be done without preliminary knowledge; and it is this knowledge which the would-be critic should set out to acquire.

3

His first step should be to ascertain that he stands clear in the intuitive conception of music and of criticism without which we shall assume that the idea of becoming a musical critic would never have entered his head. Indeed, an irresistible impulse is the sole excuse, and will in the long run prove the sole salvation, of the musical critic. But he must test every intuitive notion of his in the light of experience, with the object of determining what scope music offers to criticism, and what criticism can do with regard to music. In other words, he must begin by forming a clear idea of the work which lies before him, of the tools with which he has to do the work, and of the way in which he is to use the tools.

Forthwith the question arises, is he to consider first the work, and then proceed to equip himself with the necessary tools and decide upon a course of action ; or first the tools and what can be done with them, and then determine the direction and scope of his work according to the equipment which he finds available?

The reply would be comparatively simple if he could be certain of finding tools for all the purposes which the work may include. But it will be easy for him to see—if only by noticing the shortcomings of the very writers to whom he may turn for enlightenment—that the tools are few and in many respects inadequate ; and that it is important to make sure, before deciding upon the work to be done, that the means of doing it are at hand or can be discovered : otherwise, he may find himself in the position of a man who, having decided that he must fly, is unable to procure a flying machine, and must either give up his purpose or fling himself into mid-air towards unavoidable disaster. Moreover, to reply to this preliminary question would amount to solving practically the whole range of problems, philosophical and practical, which arise in conjunction with both music and criticism. And for this reason, even if it were possible for the critic to begin by deciding upon a certain course, it would be inadvisable to do so. Even admitting, for the sake of argument, that the course of criticism is perfectly clear and incontrovertible, the fact remains that music is an art in which there are many unknown quantities. Some writers either ignore these, or eliminate them by assuming the right to follow a system of some sort—to derive their judgements from a preconceived theory of what music is, or should be ; or to allege that individual opinion and feeling are the sole standards by which music should be judged.

To declare without further ado that these writers are wrong would be simply to follow their lead along the path of arbitrariness. And arbitrariness is the very danger against which the student should be most emphatically warned. But what we may insist upon is that they should justify their assumptions beyond the possibility of a doubt. Their labours will fall short of the mark in proportion as they fail to provide this justification.

4

If we admit that the critic's first duty is to justify his attitude and make his course of procedure clear, it means that investigation of the principles of criticism implies investigation of the principles of aesthetics— whether chiefly as a starting-point or chiefly as an element of evidence and counter-evidence, will appear shortly.)

The student who, while refraining from jumping to conclusions, considers under their most general aspect the variety of problems which lie before him before considering their application to music will find help at the very outset. For we know very little of music, and that little is almost impossible to test and is constantly liable to challenge. Writers on aesthetics in general are on far safer ground when they consider any art but music, and generally show it more or less obviously. And as we pass from aesthetics to criticism, the ground becomes even firmer—at least so long as we hold off musical criticism. Every general problem of criticism has been investigated with some thoroughness from the theoretical point of view and from the practical. Hence a further reason for considering the tools first, and the work afterwards.

Furthermore, by considering the possible application to music of the variety of solutions of each problem of criticism, we may find it easier to cast light upon the particular requirements and conditions laid down by the very nature of music.

The best thing which the student can do is to start by reading and digesting a number of standard works on the principles and methods of criticism and of standard critical essays.

A complete syllabus for this study will be found in Gayley and Scott's *Introduction to the Methods and Materials of Literary Criticism* (Boston, Ginn & Co., 1901). The one drawback, from the would-be musical critic's point of view, is that it would take several years to follow it through. What I suggest is that he should peruse it for principles, landmarks, and references, and afterwards keep it at hand and consult it freely. The sooner he begins to practise the better. But however impatient he may be, he will find that if anything can speed his course, it is precisely this book, which condenses and simplifies matters by giving full and clear statements on all points at issue and choice of solutions, as well as terse and lucid digests of books and essays which will spare him a good deal of further reading and lead him straight to what is vital (it will be necessary, of course, to include many things written after 1901). The choice lies between a certain amount of preliminary labour and an endless prospect of perplexities and sins of both omission and commission.

5

In proportion as each point is made clear, there remains to test its application to music ; to ascertain whether many things which are legitimate and useful in other branches may not prove trifling or out of place where music is concerned.

This is where it becomes necessary to delve into musical aesthetics, and where, as soon as the student is lured into following theorists upon their chosen grounds, real trouble begins.

The variety of explanations provided of the nature of music, the affinities and differences between it and other arts, the rationale of its appeal, and so forth, is endless. Most of them contain some proportion of truth, perhaps, but certainly a good deal more that is open to challenge. And, taken collectively, they constitute a mass of contradictory assertions.

Fortunately a far simpler course may serve. A fact to which everything that has been written on musical aesthetics, be it sense or nonsense, points out, is that there does exist some kind of difference between music and the other arts. Let the student, then, admit this as a working basis and, with his practical purpose in mind, try to get hold of a more definite starting-point and to proceed with as few postulates as possible (the ideal is to postulate nothing at all), guarding against hasty generalizations, and testing the ground at every step.

Instead of asking, with the builders of systems, whether music differs from other arts through having no starting-point or model in nature, or whether the difference is only apparent because music does possess some such model or starting-point, it is possible to proceed by drawing obvious, straightforward inferences from the differences between the resources and materials used by music and the other arts respectively.

The materials which the other arts use and music does not are words, shapes, lines, and colours. All these convey a meaning, definite though variable within limits, to the human intellect unassisted. And therefore the intellect naturally co-operates with the other faculties in the perception of the relationships between the several parts of the work of art, and subsequently between the parts and the whole, which are the very foundation of art and artistic pleasure.

The part thus played by the intellect is variable.

In the non-poetic types of literature it is far greater than in the poetic types, where something subtler creeps in which is precisely called 'the music' of poetry—an element of pure sound, rhythm, and proportion, as important as in painting the elements of pure design, colour, and values, apart from the tendency to represent, to describe, or to suggest ideas and associations.

But it is in the matter of painting and sculpture, perhaps, that the various aspects and stages of the co-operation stand clearest. Works of these orders originate in the contemplation of some concrete object. The senses have perceived the elements of this object-model (lines, surfaces, volumes, and colours); the intellect has determined their immediate significance (quality, form, and other attributes) and the relations between them (balance, symmetry, contrasts, &c.); and the imagination, stimulated by the mysterious thing called aesthetic emotion, has interpreted these relations so as to disengage their vital significance, their artistic import. According as the importance of the representative element in the work of art decreases, the part played by the intellect dwindles.

The materials used by music are sounds and rhythms, to which the intellect can ascribe no definite meaning except by a very questionable process of abstract association, as distinct from the concrete type of association which refers a contour or a colour to a natural object. The student will have to decide for himself what to think of the value of this process; he will probably find the evidence against it overwhelmingly strong, both on general grounds and from the particular point of view of music. But anyhow, it is safe to admit that sounds and rhythms, taken singly or in combination, cannot directly convey to the intellect a meaning such as may be conveyed by words, colours, shapes, and lines. This, for the student's purpose, is a good enough starting-point.

But we do not wish to beg the question whether the part played in determining the data from which criticism starts depends upon the meaning to the intellect of the materials which each art uses. However tempting are the reasons for believing that it is right to say that it does, we cannot ignore the fact that criticism takes a good deal into account besides materials. In music it is most important to make sure whether the intellect may validly play a part in bridging the distance from the materials to the artistic results ; for this is a point upon which much doubt seems to exist—doubt whose reasons are summed up in this sentence from Parry's *Evolution of the Art of Music* : ' in music form and design are most obviously ' necessary, because the very source and reason of the ' art is so obscure '. Of form and design—and of sounds and rhythms themselves—the intellect is able to form as clear a conception as of any concrete object or abstract idea. Upon this foundation the mind may find it possible to build ; and the notion that thereby the darkness may be dispelled, wholly or partly, finds many supporters.

This is one of the chief problems which the musical critic has to confront, and probably the most insidious. It is constantly present, and never fails to play havoc.

√The possibility of making use of whatever analogies exist between the various arts as well as of differences between them must not be lost sight of. Nor must we forget that it may lead to vagueness. ⟩ In proportion as our familiarity with the various forms of art and artistic problems increases, we learn to set greater store by everything which differentiates each art from all others, to discriminate more sharply between the appeal of music and that of painting, poetry, and the others. Correspondingly, we are led to expect that criticism will make the same differentiations. What we want to know is whether the work dealt with embodies a message worth conveying, and worth conveying in the medium and terms in which the artist elected to convey it. It is not enough that the critic should describe a piece of music or express his opinion of it in terms which, except perhaps for a few matter-of-fact particulars and a few bits of technical jargon, might as well refer to a poem, or a picture, or even a narration in the baldest prose. Nor is it enough that he should refer to a work without specifying the presence or absence, beyond the features which must be common to works of a certain order, of those features to which each work will owe its own vitality and *raison d'être*. Wherever we notice a lack of definition, we begin to wonder how far this may be due to the fundamental elusiveness of the very elements which make of each work of art a thing so special and apart, and how far to the shortcomings of the art and science of criticism. Certainly the critic should no more wish to inspire mistrust of criticism than a brewer mistrust of beer. Besides, we may also begin to wonder whether the defects are not due to the critic's own shortcomings.

8

The replies to these questions will not merely serve to determine the range which eventually the student will allow himself. This range is a matter of disposition as well as of expediency; and unless he is prepared to fight each of his battles to the finish, he has hardly any business to enter the field. These replies will point to the methods to which he had better resort, fully realizing the admissions which they imply and all the possible consequences. The better he sees that certain things may be asserted, but not proved either by evidence or by arguments, the better he will realize his problem and the extent of his responsibilities.

At this point, he will reach the conclusion that some kind of compromise must intervene. From the point of view of principle, a good many things may be understood by common consent, by a supposed tacit agreement between the critic and his readers. But if the agreement is not to be explicitly claimed by him at the outset, it should bear upon points about which no doubt can exist. In practice the one thing which the critic must fear is to deceive himself and others by being inconsistent beneath an appearance of consistency, arbitrary beneath an appearance of judicious method. Let him realize, if facts point that way, that all criticism must be tinged with prejudice of some sort, and that unprejudiced criticism, were it possible, might defeat its own ends by lacking point and driving power; that criticism, maybe, resolves itself, wholly or partly, into a matter of sympathy between the critics and the artists on one hand, the critics and their readers on the other—a sympathy affecting the emotions, the outlook, or the methods of thought.

The better he sees this, the more he will incline to put his faith in caution and consistency—the former not incompatible with daring, nor the latter with flexibility.

Arnold Schönberg (in his *Treatise of Harmony*) writes of the teacher that ' he is not the infallible, ' the man who knows everything and never errs, but ' the indefatigable who is for ever seeking and some- ' times rewarded by finding '. This is equally true of the critic. Likewise Sir Henry Hadow (*Edinburgh Review*, October 1906) writes: ' The true critic is ' simply the most enlightened listener; not standing ' aloof with a manual of arrogant imperatives, but ' taking his place among us to stimulate our attention ' where it falters, and to supplement our knowledge

' where it is deficient. We accept his judgement as
' soon as we are convinced that it illuminates the point
' at issue.'

Even with such precepts in mind, the critic will at
times elect to stand up as counsel for the prosecution
or for the defence. He will be entirely within his
rights so long as he does not delude himself or others
into believing that he is sitting as a judge. In all
cases let his attitude and his reasons for adopting it
be as unambiguous as is humanly possible. He will
then be doing as much good and as little harm as he
may hope to do. It is with this object in view that
he should start ruthlessly to analyse every point of
principle and method, to test every link in his work,
and to foresee every possible implication.

CHAPTER II

PROBLEMS OF CRITICISM IN THEIR RELATION TO MUSIC

I

No further reference will be made here to the problems dealt with in Gayley and Scott's book, except so far as it is possible to offer some definite remarks upon their application to music.

A main problem is the choice between two conceptions of criticism : one asserts that there exist certain constant standards of beauty, the critic's function consisting in discovering how far works conform to these standards ; the other denies the existence of such canons, and has its guiding principles summed up in Wordsworth's utterance that ' every great and ' original artist, in proportion as he is great and original, ' must himself create the taste by which he is to be ' relished ; he must teach the art by which he is to ' be seen '.

There may be certain constant standards of musical beauty. Indeed, it is difficult to doubt that Hadow (*Studies in Modern Music*, chap. i) has succeeded in defining them in the main. But, to quote his own words, his sole aim was to determine ' the permanent ' principles of criticism which may enable us to dis- ' criminate good from bad '. The question how to effect the discrimination remains untouched, except in one particular : the principles which he suggests (principle of vitality, principle of labour, principle of proportion, and principle of fitness) differ from the purely abstract principles laid down by builders

26

of *a priori* systems. They point to a practical application.

This, for the student, is a distinct gain. All deductive methods, upon analysis, will be found to take something for granted which begs the very questions at issue. Of these methods the least arbitrary in appearance is that which proceeds by studying a number of undisputed masterpieces with the object of discovering canons which are afterwards presented as universal and invariable. These canons may be as general as Hadow's four principles. If so, it is often necessary to eke them out by more precise stipulations before proceeding to apply them. Or they may imply restrictions of some kind. In either case, the danger is that something doubtful may be taken for granted.

We may know that music rests upon certain principles of form, design, and rhythmical balance. What these principles are we do not know except so far as we find their exemplification in particular cases. Admitting that it is in beautiful music that we can best discover the principles of musical beauty, we cannot remain blind to the fact that whenever we begin to postulate we may find ourselves confronted by the deadlock of contrary postulations.

2

This is so obvious, and the dogmatic attitude has been so thoroughly disposed of in principle, that it would have been unnecessary to comment upon it but for the fact that in practice there are more ways than one of dogmatizing. Critics do not always know when they begin to dogmatize, nor is it always easy to see when they do.

The question arises whether criticism should be judicial, deciding what is good and what is bad, or purely analytic, describing and comparing without intention to appraise.)

27

In point of fact, the distinction will be found more virtual than real. To believe that descriptive criticism, as soon as it rises above the level of pedagogic definition, may remain impassive, is a mere illusion. Turning to critics who profess not to judge, but merely to collate facts about works and tendencies, we see that their utterances, in tone and wording, always amount to judgements professed or implied. And as regards music, any description which does not contain terms amounting to actual judgements will not only fail to show whether the work possesses vitality, but also to be characteristic as a description.

Let the student try, however, if such be his choice, to stick to analytic and descriptive methods. It is capital practice. If he is endowed with the gift of self-criticism, he will learn more about the ease with which boundaries may be overstepped than he would from any amount of mere advice.

If he is in favour of judicial criticism, but realizes the advantages of the inductive methods over the deductive, there remains for him to decide between what is known as subjective criticism, which does not pretend to depend upon anything but the writer's disposition and views, and objective criticism, in which personal feeling is not taken into account, since the judgements pronounced are given as resting upon features actually presented by the works examined, or upon some equally unquestionable evidence.

Here, as everywhere, the choice will depend in no small measure upon each student's conception of the purposes of criticism, and therefore on the outcome of the investigation mapped out by Gayley and Scott in their first chapter. But it is worth while to ask ourselves what follows upon the reply to the question whether criticism should be a creative art, aiming at reproducing or otherwise transmitting the critic's vision and estimate of the works criticized, or an art of exegesis, concerned first with determining, and

28

whenever necessary showing, data and other reasons for every judgement.

Unless he thinks that intuition, unchecked and unassisted, can hold the field, the critic is bound to resort to the process of exegesis, if only for himself.

3

One supporter of the idea that criticism should be a creative art—he writes, ' an imitative art ', but in the same sense as painting is an imitative art—W. J. Blaikie Murdoch (in *Memoirs of Swinburne and other Essays*), makes an extreme case by saying that in criticism technical knowledge of subjects counts as little as it does, for instance, in painting. ' Whistler ', he says, ' was not a builder of bridges or barges : yet ' he dared depict his impressions and personal views ' of such things.'

Here we have in convenient form the replies often given to two of the most difficult questions which the critic has to confront ; for, besides the question of exegesis *versus* impressions, that of the desirability of technical knowledge is dealt with. They are not inseparable, for exegesis need not rest on a technical foundation. Indeed, to consider them jointly leads to unnecessary complications. Keeping, for the time being, to the main issue, we realize that ' imitative ' criticism must resort to some order of description, analytic or synthetic, to paraphrases whose object will be consciously or unconsciously to provide an estimate of the work under notice.

A curious result ensues. The mere fact that criticism uses the same medium—words—as the creative branches of literature (or shall it be said, in order to avoid all appearance of begging the question, as the *other* branches of literature ?) may lend an almost identical appearance of finality to the more persuasive forms of narrative or descriptive paraphrases of a picture, a poem, a statue, a piece of music. Take, for instance, Pater's famous page on *La Gioconda* (in *The Renaissance*) or Baudelaire's almost equally famous page on the *Tannhäuser* Overture (in *L'Art Romantique*), and you will see that they give interpretations of the works criticized under a form whose nature, principle, and appeal are those of a work of art. They aim at producing in a fresh medium as direct an equivalent as possible of what, in the opinion of the writers, the authors of *La Gioconda* and the *Tannhäuser* Overture had produced in their own chosen media. This means that the problems of criticism are shifted rather than solved. Apart from its persuasiveness, this type of criticism possesses no feature whose value can be ascertained except by reference to the work criticized—that is, by a critical process.

In practice, however, its value depends upon the degree of faith we place in its writer's taste, sensitiveness, knowledge, consistency, or upon the degree in which his enthusiasm (or, as the case may be, his disgust) is infectious ; it may be extremely deceptive.

A French critic (Georges Servières, I think), engaged in writing the history of the first performance at Paris of *Tannhäuser*, discovered an account, signed by an unknown journalist, which struck a note of enthusiasm and insight hardly less remarkable in its way than Baudelaire's. Further investigation revealed that this journalist noticed in similar terms of apparently judicious enthusiasm all the works performed during his term of office.

But, to revert to Mr. Blaikie Murdoch's simile, if you put a number of painters to paint the same object at the same moment you will have, after eliminating those who paint by rote or system and those who suffer from feebleness of vision or colour-blindness, or other disabilities, as many different interpretations as there remain painters. The same will happen in criticism, and there will be nothing to show which of

30

the various interpretations are anything but random shots which, as it happens, hit or miss the mark—be the mark a general truth or the reader's own point of view.

4

All this reduces itself to the question, which is the better weapon, persuasion or conviction? And the merits of exegetic methods remain to be considered. No definition of these methods is more to the point than J. M. Robertson's in his *New Essays towards a Critical Method*. It shows that persuasion is useful, but that the power to convince will achieve more.

He defines scientific criticism as ' capable of per-
' suading and convincing men by a consistent drawing
' of conclusions from premises . . . proceeding from
' points agreed on to points in dispute, and showing
' that consistency involves one view as following on
' another '.

' Progress in criticism ', he continues, ' consists in
' having a more intelligent regard to consistency alike
' in the theory and in the practice of judgement. . . .
' A twofold consistency, logical and aesthetic, is the
' test of rightness in criticism : the starting-point
' being not any absolute theory of truth or beauty,
' but just a certain measure of common opinion.'
Thus criticism becomes ' a process of circumspect
' persuasion, of reasoning from a common ground to
' a new ground, on a basis of fairly proved facts,
' setting up a basis for a certain amount of rational
' agreement among a certain number of educated
' people of different countries, interested in such a
' question ; which agreement will in turn become, so
' far as it might avail, a force in fresh criticism and
' in fresh production '.

There can be no doubt that consistency will greatly help the musical critic in the special difficulties inherent in his task. However doubtful the foundations of musical criticism, he will gain much by making clear which starting-point he adopts and justifying each step.

The 'certain measure of common opinion', the 'basis of fairly proved facts', may be found to amount to very little indeed. It may reduce itself, in Pater's words, to 'the measure of what a long experience has shown will at least never displease us': and thence to 'the art by which the great and original artist is to be seen' is a long step, especially when this artist's contribution includes much which may be at variance with what we have hitherto learnt from experience.

'The careful critic's faculty,' Robertson writes, 'be 'it great or small, is to begin with a faculty of com-'parison; he must therefore do much comparing—'comparing of works, of men, of judgements on these', with the result that he will eventually find 'the 'ostensible chaos of opinions open to some simple 'explanations which classify its forms'. He must constantly be comparing himself with himself, and his judgements with those of others.

It is in the natural order of things that there should exist as many shades of opinion—that opinion which is for ever oozing out, no matter how studiously a critic strives to be impersonal or dispassionate—as there are critics. When we say that any of these is right, we merely mean that it agrees with a measure of common opinion reached by virtue of a process of action and reaction between conflicting opinions, of attrition and elimination. When we say, 'Time is the only critic', we refer to the fact that the process must needs be gradual, and is often slow. Until it is gone through, the utmost we can do is to assume that a judgement is right, or that it is wrong. If anything can speed the process, it is comparison of judgements.

This in turn implies analysis of judgements, and no accurate analysis is possible unless judgements are

32

decomposed into their most elementary terms. There is no current aesthetic judgement which upon analysis does not resolve itself into a dozen distinct judgements if not two score. For instance, the statement that a work is beautiful contains as many judgements as we choose to acknowledge elements making for beauty : judgements referring to form and to substance, to matter and to treatment, to spirit and to effect. The more simply worded and the more general a judgement, the more complicated the process of analysis will prove to be.

When reduced to its simplest expression, every judgement will be found to refer either to a point of fact or to a point of opinion. The difference of course is that facts are invariable, and therefore of two contradictory judgements pointing to facts, one is necessarily wrong. Whether facts may be adduced in musical criticism without some sort of construction which will constitute an opinion being put upon them, will have to be ascertained. Even if it be found that in all judgements worth formulating the part played by points of fact is exceedingly small, that little will be worth having.

5

Apart from historical and biographical facts, and other elements of evidence lying outside the works considered, all the facts which concern music are in music, are music. This provides the reply to the question whether technical knowledge is of use to the musical critic.

It stands to reason that an affirmative reply does not refer to the technical knowledge which is needful to the composer. Do not let us be deluded by the similarity of the ground covered : the only thing that matters is the direction taken. The composer's object is to know how to do things, and the critic's is to know how things are. Whether he shall impart any of this knowledge to his readers, revealing the process by which he arrives at conclusions, is a matter of practice and will be duly considered by him. It has nothing to do with the question whether he needs this knowledge.

Likewise, to say that the critic must possess technical knowledge has nothing to do with the question whether technical knowledge plays a paramount part, or any part at all, in the critical operation. Technical knowledge may fail to improve the critic's capacity to disengage and interpret what is vital; but it will help him to classify his data and impressions and to state things more clearly. It is only that rudimentary form of technical knowledge which never rises beyond the capacity to find labels for things which is misleading for reader and writer alike.

What does the critic need? Obviously, the power to discriminate—which is essential—and the capacity to reduce what he discriminates to some sort of order —towards which necessary achievement the best help devised by human ingenuity is nomenclature. We do not expect anybody to be able to form an opinion of books without knowing the vocabulary and grammar of the language they are written in, nor of pictures if he cannot tell red from blue or a straight line from a circle. It does not matter two pins whether he who listens to music knows that a flute is a flute, a third a third, a Rondo a Rondo, and so on. But he must be able to derive distinct impressions, even if only unconsciously, from the tone of a flute and that of a trumpet, or the sound of a third and that of a seventh, the design of Rondo-form and that of the French Overture. He may be unable to give a name to anything he encounters at a concert or a music-shop, and yet be an excellent judge of music provided his ear, memory, and imagination are keen enough. But, exactly as for the world at large the greatest artist is not he who is endowed with the loftiest and most

34

original conceptions, but he who possesses the gift of expressing best such fine things as he conceives, so the best critic is not necessarily he who has the fullest intuition of what is conveyed by a work of art, but he who, having an adequate intuition, is best capable of expressing and justifying what he feels and thinks.

Robertson's description of the ideal critic should ever be present in the student's mind :

'A good critic, in our sense of a man with many
'forms of interest, with a manifold outlook on life, is
'by implication capable of appreciating many kinds
'of literary performance. He must be vowed to no
'artistic school, but open to the most diverse; and,
'if he have predilections, he must not insist on them
'to the disregard of excellences which come less close
'to him. . . . The critic . . . is a type with a tempera-
'ment, with prejudices or leanings of education, with
'more or less expert culture in the different matters
'with which he deals. He is thus sure sometimes to
'express a prejudice, or a limitation of sympathy, or
'an unexpert opinion; and like everybody else he is
'liable to variations of mood, which add to the pos-
'sibilities of inconsistency. Against these various
'snares he may guard with various degrees of success.
'Against the worst results of variations of mood he
'may guard by cultivating the habit of comparing
'himself with himself, of criticizing his own work.
'But as regards his limitations and his antipathies, he
'can only partially take precautions, and this only by
'a kind of discipline which few are ready to practice.
'In sum, it consists in carefully studying all the cases
'of wide appreciation in which he cannot feel with
'the many, and carefully estimating the calibre of the
'judgements with which he cannot agree. Suppose
'it be that he does not readily enjoy or admire
'Cervantes, or Calderon, or Schiller, or Hugo, or
'Browning, or Dickens, or Tolstoy, each of whom has
'won very high, and some very general, praise, it is

' his business as a scrupulous and scientific critic to
' consider closely that praise, to ask himself narrowly
' whether he has missed the excellences on which it
' dwells, to consider the training, the bias, the cast of
' mind of those who bestow it, and then, if he thinks
' he fairly can, to explain it in terms of the prejudice,
' or limitation, or deficient culture of his admirers ;
' or, if he cannot, to seek *objectively* for the merits
' which delight them, and to note those as forms of
' effect to which he is but slightly susceptible.'

Equally valuable is the writer's suggestion that ' the
' perfect scientific critic, the critic of the future per-
' haps, might be conceived as prefacing his every
' judgement—or the body of his judgements—with
' a confession of faith, bias, temperament, and training.'

He suggests that the confession might take, for
example, the following form :

' I have a leaning to what is called " exact " [*or*
' religious *or* mystical] thought, with [*or* without]
' a tenderness for certain forms of arbitrary [*or* spiritual]
' sentiment which prevail among many people I know
' and like. I value poetry as a stimulus to sympathy
' and moral zeal [*or* as the beautiful expression of any
' species of feeling], caring little [*or* much] for cadence
' and phrase as such ; accordingly I value Browning
' and Dante and Hugo above Heine and Musset and
' Tennyson [*or* vice versa]. . . . I am reverent [*or*
' irreverent] of august tradition and social propriety ;
' and I have little taste [*or* I care above all things], in
' imaginative literature, for those forms called realistic,
' as aiming at a close fidelity to everyday fact [*or* for
' those exercises of invention which carry me most
' completely out of my normal relation to my sur-
' roundings]. . . . My main physical diathesis is ——.
' Finally, I am —— years of age in this year ——.
' The dates of my essays will thus let the reader know
' how old I was when I wrote them.'

36

In point of fact, most critics, consciously or not, reveal their temperament, at least partly, at some time or other. The expert reader, when familiar with a certain critic's writings, will seldom find it difficult to detect unmistakable signs of this critic's predispositions, outlook, and possible bias. Not so, however, the average reader, at whose enlightenment and guidance the critic should sedulously aim ; nor he who reads only one article by a critic, or short notices possibly couched in most trenchant terms.

I do not suggest that every critic had better thrust a circumstantial confession upon his readers. That kind of thing, unless very well done, is apt to be very dull ; and nothing but practical experience will enable the critic to know exactly what to say in it, and how to say it. Another danger for the tiro is that either his profession of faith will be too vague, and he will be prompted by it to go on thinking loosely, or it will take the form of untested assertions—the very thing which he should most carefully shun. In fact, he will naturally tend to consider as a profession of faith that which is a mere confession, and afterwards incline to stick to his guns at all costs. As shown in chapter iv, the materials he will be dealing with do not provide the same correctives to this inclination as the materials with which other branches of criticism deal.

Generally, the more definite the statements in a confession, the likelier the critic is to find that by uttering it he has laid a rod in pickle for himself. Neither his outlook nor his practice will prove beyond challenge. But he should be prepared for this experience, and when it comes he will find it good for him.

The best way for him to outline his confession will be to investigate his would-be standards on the lines suggested in the following chapters ; to read books or essays embodying confessions or professions of faith (Hadow's opening chapters to both volumes of *Studies*

37

in Modern Music, and Parry's *Evolution of the Art of Music* and *Style in Musical Art,* will do splendidly to begin with) and try his hand at extracting from these adequate digests of their authors' beliefs, analysing without attempting, for the time being, to criticize.

Some writers have actually penned circumstantial confessions. Berlioz, for instance, in the first chapter of *A Travers Chants* (Paris, 1862), tells us exactly what he conceives music to be and in what way he responds to music. His confession is not quite full : for instance, he fails to inform us that he has a rooted objection to contrapuntal treatment—a bias which he unmistakably reveals elsewhere, and which accounts for his incapacity to respond to Bach's music, for example ; this bias compares with Mussorgsky's dislike of working out revealed both by himself in his correspondence and by an account which Borodin wrote of him. Debussy prefaced his criticisms in the French *Revue Blanche* with a declaration of principles which he reproduced later when starting to write for a Paris daily. This is published with slight modifications at the beginning of his *Monsieur Croche, Anti-dilettante* (Paris, 1921). The main ideas are that to state one's impressions is better than to criticize ; that technical analysis is doomed to futility, and that ' discipline should be ' sought in freedom, not in the formulae of decaying ' philosophies '.

The introduction and the first few essays in W. J. Turner's *Music and Life* form a very definite confession which may with excellent purpose be analysed.

What Robertson suggests is rather more than any musical critic has actually done so far. His suggestion will prove fairly easy to follow so far as concerns conscious outlook and predispositions founded upon mental idiosyncrasies, but extremely difficult when the time comes to deal with predispositions such as those examined in the following chapter. If ever the suggestion put forward (for example, by Dr. Jacob Bradford, ' Musical Criticism and Critics ', *Westminster Gazette*, vol. cxlii, No. 5) that an examination be instituted for professional musical critics materialized, a paper of that kind should certainly be included among the subjects—marks being determined, of course, by the thoughtfulness, thoroughness, and consistency of the statements, not by the writer's tendencies.

CHAPTER III

THE FIRST STEPS. STANDARDS

I

Whatever his purpose and his methods, the critic at work is influenced by a quantity of factors, some of which are components of the music he is judging (these may be named, for the sake of convenience, data), others are components of his own disposition and outlook (these may be named standards), and others are neither components of that music nor part of his individuality and artistic tenets. To this last category belongs all the information derived from historical, biographical, and other documentary sources, all the circumstantial evidence which is to be gathered from the writings and sayings of the composers themselves or of other people ; these may be grouped under the collective heading, indirect data and standards—standards remaining distinct from data, inasmuch as they are the outcome of a constructive process, as will presently be shown.

The student is requested to admit at this point that anything which is not in the music, be it an exhaustive statement of a composer's aims and methods of achieving these aims, like that of Kuhnau in his introduction to the Bible Sonatas, or a mere defining or suggestive title such as *Symphonie pathétique*, *Poème de l'Extase*, *Festklänge*, *Sarcasmes*, must be included in the third category ; and that any value which the collateral data thus provided may possess is subordinate to that of the data provided by the music. There should be little doubt that in proportion as the music thus

40

labelled is, or fails to be, pathetic, ecstatic, festive, or sarcastic in character, the label will be needless, or deceptive. On the other hand, matters become less simple with titles such as *Tamara*, or *The Pranks of Till Eulenspiegel*, or *Falstaff*. Indeed, the question whether titles of this kind, implying the existence of what is called a ' programme ', convey or do not convey information failing which it would be impossible correctly to appreciate these works, is a matter for endless discussion among aestheticians and critics. The student may begin by considering how far matters can be advanced if he restricts his attention, during the first stage of investigation, to the direct data which the music supplies.

Music consists of sounds and rhythms in a certain order of co-ordination and contrast ; by this order, relationships are established, and these constitute design and form. The bare fact of physical sensation produces certain crude, physical, unconscious reactions, and is followed by conscious perception. Upon the things thus perceived a process which depends upon aesthetic sensibility puts some sort of construction, definite, yet as indefinable in its essentials as aesthetic sensibility itself ; and other processes put other constructions which may be parallel (as when our mind discovers the reasons for which a work had struck us as beautiful or the reverse) or divergent (as when we are instinctively attracted by a work, and our mind discovers reasons for correcting this impression). How far these processes intermingle, which takes place first, and which has or should have the casting vote, are so many vexed questions.

2

Under ideal conditions, the problem how to arrive at a critical estimate of music would be simple enough. As Hadow puts it (*Studies in Modern Music*, ii. 75) : ' For the proper appreciation of musical excellence,

' there are no strange or recondite qualities demanded :
' only receptivity of ear, only sanity of emotion, only
' patience that is willing to observe, and courage that
' is ready to speak its mind. The rest is a matter of
' training and experience : training by which we
' rouse our faculties to a higher stage of development,
' experience by which we learn to equip our criticism
' with new facts and new relations.' To this list of
requisites should be added, of course, imagination, the
sine qua non of the capacity to enjoy any form of art.
And the student will find it useful to investigate in
due time the exact meaning that should be ascribed
to the term ' sanity of emotion '. (This, again, is not
a problem which a tiro may hope to solve, as shown
by the fact that criticism has freely described as
' morbid ' admiration for Chopin, Wagner, Tchaikovsky, Debussy, Richard Strauss, and Schönberg.)
In practice the complex elements which constitute
aesthetic appreciation are never independent of each
listener's personal equation. This is no drawback
from the point of view of the listener, nor yet, in
principle, from that of the critic ; but it is something
of which he should be constantly aware, so as to be on
his guard against its possible consequences.

In all other respects, the difference between the
professional and the layman is one of degree and not
of kind. Both are in the same position as regards the
music they are listening to and trying to form an
opinion of. Only the critic, perforce, is more conscious ; and he needs to be trained to develop and
control his impulses, to know as exactly as possible
which construction he puts on his perceptions, how
he puts it, and why.

With regard to this knowledge, the influence and
memory of past experiences plays an all-important
part ; a part so obviously legitimate and necessary
(especially if we admit with Robertson that ' criticism
starts with a faculty of comparison '), that he may

42

incline to trust to this memory unreservedly, and sometimes uncritically.

Having determined that the critic's building materials and tools are primarily the data and standards provided by (*a*) the music, (*b*) his idiosyncrasies, and (*c*) his experience, and decided to defer a while all questions of collateral information, we may dispose, so far as possible, of the question of idiosyncrasies; for these affect both the way in which the critic reacts to music and the way in which he acquires and uses his knowledge.

3

Idiosyncrasies are difficult to disengage in practice. Now and then, however, it becomes possible to get a glimpse of some particular tendency at work singly. If the student agrees with the overwhelming majority of writers who have made their mark in aesthetics, he will probably have discarded all tendencies by virtue of which works of art are judged otherwise than as ends in themselves—with reference, say, to the alleged moral or social functions of art. However, a particularly insidious form (insidious because it may appear to conform entirely with the requirements of the aesthetic sense) of the habit of judging musical works with regard to their function in the evolution of music will have to be considered separately.

Some of the critic's idiosyncrasies of feeling and outlook belong to what is generally called his taste— a convenient and unequivocal term, emphasizing the relativity of all that it covers. But others are sometimes considered as matters not of taste, but of common sense and logic: perhaps quite rightly so far as they originate in a certain turn of mind, inborn or acquired, and not merely in a certain humour, an emotional or imaginative disposition.

All of us naturally tend to prefer, for reasons of interest or of sympathy, certain art forms, methods, and ideals to certain others. Sympathy is a thing of the feelings, interest a thing of the intellect. The distinction is of very slight importance for the critic's purpose. Both may be inborn or acquired, and in either case modifiable by education, by other people's suggestions or appeals. There is reason to presume, however, that acquired tastes are more easily modified than inborn tastes; and that in extreme cases, attempts deliberately to acquire, alter, or suppress proclivities are carried out at the expense of genuineness, and lead to mere pretence or self-deception.

But the questions whence idiosyncrasies originate, how far their origin affects their value, and how far each one of them is modifiable, may wait. What should be noticed forthwith is the difficulty for the would-be judge of music to realize how great a part they will ever play in the formation of his judgements. This will be made clear by comparing the profession of faith outlined by Robertson for the use of literary critics with any form which a similar profession by a musical critic may take. And it is the materials for this profession which we are now attempting to discover.

4

The range of musical preferences extends from the crudest to the most subtle, and naturally the subtlest are the most difficult to study, whereas comparatively little good accrues from the study of the others.

The following remarks will appear superfluous to the man who feels assured that he likes everything which is good of its kind and knows it when he hears or reads it. He stands in no need of help, because on his own showing he commands the very secret of which we are attempting to discover at least some part. This book, or any other on the same topic, will be as useless to him as a treatise on aviation to a bird. Let those who are not so fortunate consider a few types of preferences founded on interest or on sympathy, which in turn will serve as landmarks for a further study of the matter. First, for instance, those that refer to the sensory properties of music.

Obviously we need not take protoplasmic types into account. People who prefer vocal music to instrumental, the full orchestra to the string quartet, or vice versa, people who can enjoy a beautiful voice or a beautiful tone on the violin even when the music sung or played is bad or the interpretation unintelligent, are very far from the time when they might begin profitably to consider questions of criticism. But in certain preferences which may appear no less crude in principle, there may be more than meets the eye. Take, for instance, susceptibility to volume of sound. To a listener endowed with delicately poised sensibility, volume, like everything else in music, is entirely a matter of proportion. For certain people, however, it appears to assume an absolute, not a relative, importance. A case in point is Berlioz, who wrote (*A Travers Chants*, p. 9):

'If one member of a big group of church singers 'gives out a simple theme, slow in tempo and not 'very interesting *per se*, however beautiful his voice 'and artistic his singing, the effect will be poor; but 'the same theme, repeated less artistically *unisono* by 'all, will assume an incredible majesty.'

And elsewhere, referring to Mozart's use of a solo trombone in the *Tuba Mirum* of his *Requiem*:

'Poor Mozart, who is content with a single trombone 'when five hundred would have been hardly sufficient !'

Likewise colour is so important to certain types of listeners, that it will compensate weakness of design. Others are not blinded by it, but cannot do without it : design alone will not satisfy them. For others design is all that matters, and colour does not count at all. There exist people who ascribe a great impor-

45

tance to a strong rhythmic appeal, to the appeal of pace, to smoothness of texture and contour, and so forth. There are people to whom actual physical impressions mean very little.

A particular instance may be adduced further to illustrate the infinite variety of likes and dislikes whose origin is partly, if not wholly, physical : Berlioz's attitude towards chromaticism. Even if his own music were not available to show that his ear and taste ever leaned towards the diatonic, his writings would suffice to convince us of the fact. He describes the *Tristan* Prelude as ' a long piece whose sole theme is ' a kind of chromatic wail, and which teems with dis- ' cords whose sting is increased by protracted appoggia- ' turas ' (*A Travers Chants*, p. 297). To him sequences of diminished sevenths are ' bunches of serpents that writhe and hiss and tear one another ' (ibid., p. 301).

Is there such a thing as absolute musical ugliness, or does the term ugly merely constitute the statement of a preference, mental or physical, instinctive or acquired ?

Without anticipating the solution which the student will ultimately adopt, we may presume that this solution will not altogether refuse a part to physical propensities. Sir Charles Stanford has alleged (*Proceedings of the Musical Association*, 1922, pp. 27–40) that fifths ' are as ugly now as they ever have been, ' as they ever will be, world without end . . . because ' their ugliness most probably depends upon natural ' phenomena and not upon individual taste '. Obviously, Berlioz was no less sure that the ugliness of the *Tristan* harmonies and of sequences of diminished sevenths was not a matter of individual taste, although he expressed his views in the first person. We have long since discovered that Berlioz's views on the point are not universally endorsed as all absolute truths should be ; and as regards the question of fifths, the very variety and discrepancy of the explanations offered

46

in order to account for their alleged ugliness (see Watt, *Foundations of Music*) and the fact that history shows how greatly the attitude of musicians towards fifths has varied in the course of time, prove that the not uncommon assertion here quoted in Stanford's words is questionable. It is the critic's and every listener's lot to have to encounter a good deal of music which will try the ear, at times very sorely. The ear, as we know, is essentially susceptible to education ; the average ear nowadays accepts without a qualm things that were intolerable to the average ear of a few decades ago. But with regard to any particular point, be it chromaticism, or fifths, or consecutive ninths, or the atonality and polytonality of to-day, certain ears need education and are modifiable by it, others do not need it, others remain unaffected by it. It is therefore safe to admit that the matter is, at least partly, one of natural physical disposition.

5

Not originating in physical predisposition, but equally inborn, are tastes referring to manner, diction, and style—tastes which are not, like those previously mentioned, more or less special to the appreciation of music (and of poetry so far as poetry is music) but affect the appreciation of all arts : the preference for the epic or the elegiac, for the austere or the sensuous, for exuberance or restraint, for simplicity or elaboration. The effect of such tastes is especially difficult to detect and control.

This is where the essential fact that the art of music has no obvious connexion with a starting-point in nature carries weight. Where an object-model exists, its function in the matter of appraisement is to provide, between the objective fact of the work and the subjective fact of the impression which this work creates, a third term which is useful for purposes of analysis and comparison. The part it plays in actual

47

appreciation may be very small.   It is almost generally admitted now that all the object-model may do is to enable us ' to refer the forms back to something we ' have already seen, so as to grasp more easily their ' aesthetic relations in the artist's work ' (Clive Bell, *What is Art?* p. 225).

But in criticism, comparison with the object-model may help to provide a satisfactory definition for every term employed.   Should it fail to do so, the conclusion that the critic and his reader are not on common ground may become obvious.

Surely it is very much easier to agree on the distinction between restraint and dryness, forcefulness and sensationalism, abundance and redundance, sweetness and mawkishness, in the matter of poems and paintings than in that of music, because the very definition of such qualities and defects can be illustrated by clear examples.   This is impossible in music, where the nearest approach to an object-model or third term of comparison is an ideal conception which either pre-exists in our mind (as a result of instinct, experience, system, or mere habit) or is suggested by contact with a work—as certainly occurs when we feel that a work having aroused our expectations, fulfils them or fails to fulfil them.

There is no art which invites critics so definitely as music to ignore side-issues and stick to the main point, namely, the works as they stand.   This, however, is difficult for most people and impossible for some.   It appears to be an ideal, approachable but never fully achieved.   Hence so many attempts to discover an object-model or some acceptable substitute, whether metaphysical postulates, or the Spencerian principle that music is but an idealization of the natural language of emotion, or the purely metaphorical comparisons with architecture or mathematics, or the investigation of acoustics—which are about as useful for the appreciation of music as optics are for the appreciation of

48

painting.   Hence the usually acknowledged need for
laws and standards of some kind.

For us the question is one not of challenging the
right of existence of any such law or standard, but of
ascertaining how far each law is universally valid.   In
other words, when we say ' no art without restraint ',
or ' no beauty without some strangeness in its pro-
portions ', or ' no art without reality, without human
interest, without detachment from human interests ',
and so forth, how far are we formulating laws, and
how far mere views ?

6

It may be questioned whether even these rudimentary standards originate purely in taste.   But there
can be no doubt that the main standards of criticism,
whose origin is definitely traceable to the emotions,
the intellect, and the imagination, may be more usefully discussed from the point of view of logic and
common sense even if they are not altogether matters
of common sense and logic.   The boundary is not
easy to determine.   For instance, the tendency to
dismiss fifths and chromatic effects as ugly may be
defended on mere grounds of physical unpleasantness,
which is a matter of opinion.   But the word ugly
may have (and often has in this very case) another
meaning.   It may imply that such things offend the
laws of artistic fitness ; and then the judgement is
given as founded, not on mere taste, but on an
incontrovertibly true principle.   The conscious mind
has come into operation and pronounced.

Even if it is justifiable to isolate a standard for
purposes of analysis, no useful discussion is possible if
we fail to take into account all the factors which lead
to a pronouncement.   And there are times when the
task of disengaging them all appears almost hopeless.

It is necessary to learn to determine the respective
parts played in the formation of aesthetic judgements

D

by the three orders of standards which we are now studying. But at this stage the student need not dwell long upon those standards which originate in the emotions and the imagination. With regard to these, all that one may hope to provide is a number of definitions, more or less loose, and a few landmarks. Two questions arise : quantity and quality. The former is definitely one of taste. Certain people are sensitive to the emotional properties of music only. The more definitely and emphatically emotional they find a piece of music, the better they like it. Others take into account a good many other things, and may be repelled rather than attracted by an overbalance of emotion.

At this point a confusion will arise unless we are very careful to discriminate between the general sense of the word emotion in psychological science and its specialized sense in the current language.

The former sense covers all reactions of the sensibility, conscious or not, irrespective of degree and kind, vague or definite, productive or not of pleasure, pain, images, and associations. The latter sense covers merely special affective conditions, under which the feelings are actually stirred, given a definite direction, and perhaps confirmed by some by-play of thought and imagination.

7

The qualitative problem that occurs with regard to the emotional functions of music has given rise to countless books, chapters, essays, and rhapsodies, but may be summed up in a very few words. Is music ' a pure art with a tremendous significance of its own and no relation whatever to the significance of life ' ? (Clive Bell, *What is Art?* p. 31). Should music be an object of emotion or a means of suggesting emotion? In either case, is it true that music may give rise to indefinite emotions only? Are we to admit

50

that ' the higher, more developed musical type (of
' listener) is the one who is primarily sensitive to the
' sounds and not to the emotions . . . the emotional
' listener really misses all that distinguishes music from
' any other art . . . it is the hall-mark of bad music,
' as of bad art generally, that it is emotional ' ? (W. J.
Turner, *Music and Life*, pp. 3, 4, 7).

The first two questions concern the distinction
between aesthetic emotion and all other emotions.
The second, especially, leads us to consider whether
aesthetic emotion is an end in itself, and shows the
direct consequence of an affirmative reply on this
point. If we do not admit that music is valuable as
a means of conveying emotions other than purely
aesthetic emotion, we understand why music which
moves certain listeners deeply is dismissed by certain
others as mere emotional drivel. For some critics,
the distinction is a matter of degree ; but for others
it is one of principle.

The third question, which we frequently encounter
in writings on music, may be taken to exemplify the
dangers of side-issues introduced by vagueness of ideas
or of vocabulary. It may be that ' indefinite emotions ' means emotions in the scientific sense, as distinct
from the ' definite ' emotions implied by the word in
its current sense : in which case we are brought back
to the question whether the emotions aroused by music
are definable in terms of human experience outside
art. It is upon this doubtful issue that the greater
part of the discussions on the value of ' programme
music ' originates.

The fourth question can only be understood if the
word ' emotion ' is taken in its current sense, not in
the scientific : when it will be seen that it constitutes
another version of the first but enriched by additions
which provide useful points for investigation.

All arguments in favour of emotional appreciation
are summed up in this passage by Dr. F. H. Hayward

(quoted in Mr. Percy A. Scholes's pamphlet *Musical Appreciation in Schools*, p. 14):

'. . . Two significances are better than one, and
' three than two. . . . If hearing the first movement
' of the *Fifth Symphony* we obtain (from its main
' theme) merely the sense of something impetuous,
' and do not hear the hammer-strokes of Fate knocking
' at Beethoven's door and saying " you shall suffer—
' suffer—suffer—you shall be deaf as a stone—you shall
' never know domestic joys . . ." . . . we miss much
' that it is a thousand pities to miss.'

Let the student ask himself whether this view can
be right, and whether in proportion as we allow it to
predominate we do not run the risk of ' missing all
that distinguishes music from any other art '. Let
him also notice that to accept the form given by
Dr. Hayward to his utterance (one among thousands)
is to admit that outside information (what we have
called indirect standards) may play a direct part in
aesthetic appreciation. For surely, music in itself is
incapable of foretelling the coming or the lack of
domestic joy. We all know, it is true, that it may
bring suffering if not foretell it; but we shudder
to think of the only way in which it may bring
a prospect of deafness.

8

Psychological and psycho-physiological sciences give
all needful information about emotions but very little
about imagination. Even an expert specialist like the
French philosopher Ribot finds himself compelled to
acknowledge (*Essai sur l'Imagination créatrice*, 1908,
pp. 149–51) that a satisfactory determination of the
various types of imagination is not yet possible.

It is useful to note, however, that he distinguishes
two main types: the ' plastic ', whose materials are
definite images, and in which associations are governed
by objective relationships, easily determinable; and the

' diffluent ', characterized by vague imagery and looser associations. The basis of the former is mainly sensory, but at times the affective elements balance the sensory. Another essential character is the tendency to transpose sonorous sensations and images into visual and spatial images. A less complex form of this type, he tells us, is purely rationalistic imagination ; its imagery tends towards abstraction, and its associations are the outcome of the logic of the mind rather than of the logic of the sentiments. And diffluent imagination he defines as dealing with images which are ' half-way ' between the realistic images of the plastic type and the semi-schematism of the rationalistic '. Its associations are essentially subjective, determined at times by an intellectual operation, but more often by chance ; and among its materials are images of a special kind, ' emotional abstracts ', which ' accrue from some pre- ' dominating affective condition, are temporary or ' permanent, and consist merely of certain properties ' or attributes of the things considered, disengaged so ' as to stand for the whole of these things ' (ibid., p. 164).

Slow or swift, temperate or wayward, inclining towards the abstract or the concrete, endowed with a capacity, great or small, for association and dissociation, for analysis or synthesis, the imagination sets standards of appreciation which are, when all is said and done, the determining factors of aesthetic judgements.

The bearing of all these forms and shades of imagination upon music provides a difficult but fascinating study. Alone, intuition, the highest and determining factor, baffles analysis.

9

It will be seen that in musical criticism as in most things, the functions of pure intellect are not altogether separable from those of the emotions and of the imagination. Definition and certain points of further investigation are rendered easier by dissociations, but the help thus afforded is only temporary.

Nor is it needful to carry on the study of the functions of the mind separately : its predispositions and conscious operations are better studied in conjunction with the data upon which it works, as the next chapter will attempt to show.

It is not suggested that predispositions should be considered as a necessary evil. Most of them are neither good nor bad in themselves, and some are excellent. It is only overbalance of one or several that is dangerous. Whether a perfect balance has ever existed in a human being is doubtful. But what the student can and must do is to study the influence of predispositions on his own criticism and on that of other people. Thus he will resist the temptation to judge works by the presence or absence of features which he inclines to like or dislike, and be forewarned against the risk of crediting works which he likes with features which they do not include.

CHAPTER IV

THE DATA. THE FUNCTIONS
OF THE MIND

I

COMING into contact with works, the critic sometimes finds some of his predispositions negligible and
some of his preconceived notions upset. He will like
certain works which do not conform with his preferences, and fail to like other works although they
do. This will result partly from the impressions
created by the play of his mind and the control which
his mind exercises over his other impressions, and
partly from the play of his imagination. It is here
that the critical operation proper begins. A critic to
whose experience surprises of this order are altogether
foreign must be either endowed with almost preter-
natural wisdom or unfit for his calling.

What happens is that the critic hears the music and
perceives between its various components relationships
to which he ascribes a value; or conversely he may
fail to perceive any relationships to which he can
ascribe a value. This, we know, is the uniform
principle of all aesthetic judgements.

Taken singly, the elements of music, that is, sounds,
produce a purely sensory impression. But even this
impression is often accompanied by associations : for
example, our intellect and imagination will place
different constructions on notes sounded on a violin,
a trumpet, a kettledrum respectively, on shrill notes
and on deep, on faint notes and loud. The reason lies
in our previous experience, which likewise will lead
most of us to ascribe to any note we hear a musical

55

function, a place in a scale or system of notes—to consider it, in the language of theory, as a tonic or a dominant or whatever it may be. So that even this simplest of instances shows the co-operation between all the faculties which play a part in aesthetic judgement. When sounds are combined, the relationships created by variety of pitch, intensity, duration, and colour, and by the various conditions of texture and design inherent in music, give rise to a similar co-operation on an infinitely greater scale.

Sounds and rhythms provide a cognitive element, definite, abstract, capable of fully satisfying the requirements of the intellect. This character of abstractness and definiteness naturally gives rise to the temptation to judge these relationships finally, if not solely, from the point of view of the mind, and seems to justify it. The arithmetical relations between sounds, the possibility of reducing all musical forms to diagrams, and resorting to countless other modes of classification would increase this temptation even without the help of the metaphors which the language of analysis and criticism must perforce include. Indeed, if it is true that poetry and the fine arts, by virtue of what we have called their object-models, seem to afford a far greater field to the exercise of the intellect, it is no less true that it appears easy to discover an all-embracing rationale of the otherwise indefinable relationships constituting music, whereas it is difficult to discover a rationale of this order in these other arts. How far the discovery will actually serve the critic's purpose remains to be ascertained.

2

There is no need to waste time in considering, as some writers have done, what might occur if music were judged apart from any reference to previous experiences, since the critic is bound to have had previous experiences, and it is inconceivable that these

56

should not exercise some kind of influence. What should be of interest to us is the different ways in which they affect different people. On one hand they may develop our receptiveness and perceptiveness, our flexibility and discrimination ; on the other, they may beget certain habits affecting both mind and sensibility.

In the former respect, their influence is altogether good ; in the latter, it is good only inasmuch as it shortens the process of reducing our impressions and thoughts to order, but bad inasmuch as it creates a routine.

The French philosopher Maine de Biran (*Mémoire sur l'Habitude*) has shown that habit affects our active and our passive faculties in opposite fashions, strengthening the former and weakening the latter ; this statement has never been superseded or even challenged. Emotions are essentially passive ; and here the danger of habits is that they may set the emotional processes, which then will cease to arise except automatically, under determinable circumstances (thence it occurs that certain people are unaffected, or unpleasantly affected, by all music which does not conform with a certain routine) ; or that they may so far blunt the sensibility that only the egregious will arouse it (hence the thirst for novelty at all costs and for its own sake—which is so prominent a feature at the present moment).

The intellect and imagination should be essentially active, but may under the influence of habit lose their activity and acquire a tendency to work as automatically as the emotions. And when this stage is reached, the fact that their operation usually remains conscious prevents some people from realizing it. The tendency to follow, in appraising music, the line of least resistance, dismissing as futile all that is not easy to grasp, and the opposite tendency to believe that in music all that is simple and obvious is futile, must be classed among predispositions.

57

In music what we call data (i. e. sounds, rhythms, and all the patterns and forms resulting from their combination) provide the only ground common to all people. They are as unmistakable as the subject-matter is in literature or in painting. We may differ regarding their logical function or their aesthetic interest, exactly as in other arts we may argue about points of treatment ; but we can no more deny that a fifth is a fifth, a triad a triad, a spondaic metre spondaic, and ternary form ternary (a B element being sandwiched between two A elements) than we can deny the representation of a woman in *La Gioconda*, of three men and a snake in the *Laocoön* group, the existence of Prospero, Caliban, Ariel, and Miranda in the *Tempest*, or the fact that in *The Raven* the construction centres around the repetition of the word ' Nevermore '.

If this statement be accepted (but the student will find a useful exercise in asking himself how far it and the ensuing discussion may smack of sophistry) it remains to ascertain whether more valid critical results may accrue from considering data in music than from considering the subject-matter *per se* in other arts.

We can generally find in any music some tangible features to account for our opinion of it. Judging a work monotonous, we may find an explanation provided by the lack of variety in colour, vocabulary, and thematic treatment ; judging it original, we may pounce upon facts such as the novel use of familiar means, or the use of new means ; judging it coherent in form, we may confirm our view by referring to the tonal and structural balance, to points of working out, and so on. Indeed, it is very difficult to imagine a case when no explanation of this kind can be plausibly devised.

The means by which composers have achieved

eurythmy, logic, and continuity of interest are never impossible to determine as means any more than the means by which they have achieved single effects. But in proportion as these means are known, they lend themselves to codification, of which the result may be to determine laws, to formulate rules, or merely to provide recipes, accessorily showing the way towards further rules and recipes. Is it always possible to ascertain the difference between conforming to laws, obeying rules, and following recipes? Do any such things as indubitable and invariable laws exist in music, or rather, do we positively know of any? If any exist, can they be expressed, and can their consequences be determined, in terms of the intellect?

4

To argue about the ways in which artistic creation achieves results that seem to betoken the existence of laws in music will not help us here. What will help us is to know how these laws are disengaged from these results, and thus made available for critical purposes.

There can be no doubt that the process is, at the start, empirical, and when it ceases to be empirical becomes either inductive or deductive. If inductive, the laws of music will be similar to those of the natural sciences, which are subject to modification in proportion as phenomena crop up which they do not account for.

It has been remarked that ' new theories and laws ' do not necessarily disprove old ones, but explain ' certain discrepancies in them and penetrate more ' deeply into their underlying principles. To follow ' the new reasoning, we must rid ourselves of the ' prejudice behind the old, not because it is wrong, ' but because it is insufficient ' (Bird, *Relativity and Gravitation*, p. 28).

This is true enough as regards musical laws. But

it is no less true that there exists a school of criticism which denies the possibility of modifying these laws beyond a certain point. We have to see whether this possibility may be denied except by doing what was done in the early days of the natural sciences : distorting or ignoring facts when they failed to conform with alleged laws.

If the process becomes deductive, we must remember that deduction always resorts to syllogism, and that the first condition of syllogism is that its premisses be universal. In order to found a syllogism on an empirical basis, we must begin by showing beyond the possibility of a doubt that this rule of logic is not infringed.

If our premisses are that ' sounds and patterns in music must be related to one another ', we are on safe ground. But these premisses are too vague to be of use without some kind of addition. And it is when we consider possible additions that the trouble begins.

If we say, for instance, ' sounds and patterns in ' music must be related to one another according to ' the principles which govern the relations of sounds ' in the major and minor scale as shown by current ' theory ', we begin by assuming what we may be requested to demonstrate before we venture to condemn as illogical a work in which the condition is not observed.

If we substitute a formula such as ' according to ' the principles which govern the practice of great ' masters, to wit A, B, C, D, &c.', we must again show that the practice of X, whose works might be condemned on the strength of the axiom thus modified, should not be taken into account as well as the practice of A, B, C, D, and so forth. This we may be able to show at the time when a critical estimate of X's contribution has been arrived at, but not before. Meanwhile, we shall be assuming precisely what we set out to prove.

However, if a critic is fortunate enough to hit upon premisses which are universal, altogether beyond challenge, and specific enough to provide an infallible standard of judgement, he is justified in pronouncing accordingly.

5

It is instructive to see how rules or laws may spring up in equally satisfactory form from a purely logical process and from purely experimental observation. For instance, it stands to reason that no great variety of musical metre is possible where only one metrical value is used, and that under such circumstances melodic interest may flag. It is quite true that it would be hard to discover a good melody of any great length consisting entirely of equal notes. But even in so obvious a case theory may come to grief. If we assert, as Rimsky-Korsakof does (*Principles of Orchestration*, p. 148), that ' a good vocal melody should consist of notes of at least three different values ' and omit the saving clause ' except in particular cases ' (which, by the way, he introduces only with reference to instrumental melodies), our rule lies at the mercy of any composer who will write a good melody in which three different values of notes do not appear.

As it happens, Gustav Holst has written a song (the second in his op. 35) in which only two values of notes are used. If we agree that this fact does not constitute the ultimate test of the song's goodness or badness, we must admit that the rule is neither more nor less useful than would be a rule saying that ' a good ' melody should not comprise more than twelve, or ' eighteen, or thirty-seven different values of notes '.

When Professor H. J. Watt writes (' Rule and Law in Music,' *Music and Letters*, vol. iii, No. 4, p. 351): ' If you take 50 or 100 song-melodies from any ' classical writer, . . . you will probably find . . . that ' the smallest interval of the semitone occurs most 'frequently, the interval of a tone a little less frequently, 'the minor third much less frequently, and so on', he is resorting to experimental observation. In the same article he writes : 'The essential feature of melody, 'apart from its form, is the quality of motion it 'embodies, the sense of movement from note to note 'that it assures. Now in this respect a melody is the 'more cogent the shorter the steps of pitch separating 'each note from the next.' Thus he leads us by a different route towards the conclusion which the statement quoted first points at. After having tested the logical process by which he disengages this principle of cogency, we may agree with him in admitting that this conclusion constitutes 'a highly probable rule or law'. But even with the cumulative weight of the other arguments and provisions in his article, it is impossible to admit the universality of the rule which one might be tempted to formulate in terms such as 'a good melody should comprise a majority of short intervals'. For before that statement appears in print, there is a risk that a composer will have written a good melody which does not.

When Dr. R. Felber tells us (*Zeitschrift für Musik*, September 1922) that 'moods of joy and exhilaration 'may exist in tonal music only, never in atonal music, 'because atonal music must needs sound mournful', he may mean that he has never encountered atonal music which did not sound mournful, or that he has discovered a method of demonstrating the incompatibility between atonal music and a certain order of suggestions.

His assertion bears a curious family likeness to this other older one, that 'the minor mode expresses moods of sadness'. It may serve to show that pursuers of musical laws are not always content with sober assertions such as Rimsky-Korsakof's, for which quite a fair case can be made, or cautious hypotheses such as Professor Watt's.

62

The evolution of laws in music may be divided into four distinct stages:

1. Creative artists, intent on achieving unity and other elements of artistic significance, resort to certain practices which become more usual and more definite in proportion as they prove suitable as means towards an end (whether they have been discovered by one composer or evolved by common action makes no difference). A selective and organizing process takes place.

2. The process is so far effected that theorists are able to distinguish laws and from these to devise rules. Most of these rules are in accordance with the general practice. The knowledge that the means discovered may achieve the desired end has become common property.

3. The notion becomes current among theorists and their followers that practice must conform to these rules. Meanwhile creative artists discover new means. The rules may or may not be invalidated. But the only reason for admitting the existence of actual laws —the practice of composers—is no longer perfectly satisfying. The rules subsist, but as a number of items in a modifiable whole, or with reference to certain recognized types of music.

4. The rules become mere recipes for composing or judging, whose inanity is patent to all except slaves of habit or of system.

The more general a rule is, the less the danger of its degenerating into a mere recipe, but the greater the difficulty of determining whether it has reached this stage or is in danger of reaching it.

A few concrete examples will make the above points clear.

Practice led composers to achieve variety of rhythm by changes of duration, order by limitation and recurrence of such changes. Eventually, the 8-bar phrase with its antecedents and consequents was established, in accordance not only with the general principle of order but with the less general principle of symmetry. Thus was provided a useful rule, elastic enough to endure unbroken, at least in appearance, for a long time. Enter theory, which declares the rule indispensable, while composers conform to it or neglect it according to the promptings of their creative instinct. That the notion dies hard is proved by Riemann's contention that phrases which do not actually consist of eight bars should be understood either as truncated (he tells us, for instance, that the first bar of the C minor prelude of the *Wohltemperirte Klavier*, first book, is in reality a fifth bar, the previous four being understood) or as extended by repeated bars and other devices.

Here we have all four stages in a nutshell. It is not unreasonable to suppose that should a believer in this way of applying theory encounter a musical phrase which no effort of dialectic can refer to the 8-bar type, he will be tempted to give it a bad name.

Tonality, again, was established by a gradual process.[1] Unity of scales in each key, balance of keys in musical structure, reproducing on broader lines the balance which gives its unity to each key, become the rule ; but composers extend this rule faster than theorists are able to follow them. Nowadays music has reached a stage at which tonality and the ensuing structural principles are often either extended almost beyond recognition or entirely discarded. But criticism is still guided at times by the rule that occurs, in words repaying study in more ways than one, in Parry's article on Tonality in Grove's *Dictionary*

[1] The fact that the principle of tonality may be referred to the phenomena of acoustics is not enough to justify its being raised to the dignity of a law. Indeed, the very acceptance of the principle of temperament proves that the law need not be taken literally.

64

(vol. v, p. 119) : 'Unless the tonality is made intelligible, a work which has no words becomes obscure.'

The clause ' which has no words ' is very instructive. It shows the tendency, in certain types of mind, never to judge music except by reference to some third term of comparison, which must needs consist of something cognitive ; and how, failing the existence of an actual cognitive element (such as might be provided, we are told, by words), a substitute is sought in some kind of systematized notion which the mind can fully embrace—here tonality, elsewhere the model 8-bar phrase and the various structural plans derived from it.

Lest it be thought that too much stress is laid here upon an incidental remark, let the above sentence be compared with the sentence from the same writer's *Evolution of the Art of Music* previously quoted (p. 6).

A similar tendency accounts for this assertion of Professor Klauwell's (*Geschichte der Programm-Musik*, Leipzig, 1910—only one instance among many provided by this book) :

' In Beethoven's Sonata, op. 81 *a*, the coda of the ' first movement contains a feature (the coincidence ' of the tonic sixth G–E flat with the dominant fifth ' B flat–F) which cannot be understood except by ' reference to a " programme ".' Again a mind is caught in the act of seeking for an indirect standard in preference to forgoing the cognitive term of comparison which it fails to find in its cut-and-dried notion of tonality.

And this is perhaps the sole reason why musical laws are so persistently sought for and put into requisition.

The desire to bring musical criticism under the jurisdiction of the mind is easy to account for. If this were possible, it would do away with the vagueness and uncertainty which are, beyond a certain point, inseparable from all other courses of procedure. At one end, there would be the unmistakable facts of music ; at the other, the mind, of which every step can be followed and accounted for. And should a writer, telling us that somebody or other's music is nonsense, vouchsafe no further explanation than 'that it does not make sense', we might be ready to admit that he had done enough.

This indeed is implicitly acknowledged even by critics who in theory incline to deny it. Hadow writes (*Studies in Modern Music*, ii, p. 14): Most 'vital . . . is the rational or logical side, through 'which we appraise an artistic work . . . by some 'definite and intelligible scheme of aesthetic laws.'

But he does not allow his criticism to be swayed by purely rational considerations. Speaking of 'the 'mediocrity which mistakes craftsmanship for inspira-'tion', he points out that 'men like Hummel and 'Czerny copied the design (of Sonata) but left the 'poetry out'—which is hardly demonstrable from a purely rational point of view, without an appeal to the imagination.

In truth, he distinguishes between 'discursive intel-lect, which is logical, inferential, ratiocinative', and a 'faculty of pure intuition', which 'we cannot define or describe' and 'whose one function in music is the immediate apprehension of vitality in the best work'.

To admit both faculties under one heading is a matter of mere nomenclature, but may lead to ambi-guity precisely where ambiguity is least desirable. It is clear that intuition—or, as we may elect to call it, imagination—and not discursive intellect is respon-sible for Hadow's view that the beauty of Debussy's *Pelléas et Mélisande* 'is as inexplicable as it is literally 'beyond question. We may take it or leave it, but 'we cannot analyse or discuss. The discords—so to 'call them—of which its texture is mainly composed 'are such as to have no name and no designation: 'they are so far from being justified by the gram-'marian that they cannot even be convicted by him.'

66

In the Introduction, he continues, 'there is a passage
' in whose phraseology the laws of syntax are ignored.
' Yet the effect of it, as of the whole opera, is in-
' describably charming' (*Edinburgh Review*, October
1906, pp. 385 and 391).

The same remark applies to this splendid piece of
criticism, which occurs in his Essay on Chopin (*Studies
in Modern Music*, ii, p. 163) :

' In the twelfth bar of the well-known Nocturne in
' E flat (Op. 9, No. 2) there is a connecting passage
' which, when we see it on paper, seems to consist of
' remote and recondite modulations. When we hear
' it played in the manner which Chopin intended, we
' feel that there is only one real modulation, and that
' the rest of the passage is an iridescent play of colour,
' an effect of superficies, not an effect of substance.'

Here, after the intellect has had its say (in the first
sentence), imagination steps in and says the only thing
that matters, incidentally defining a principle of
aesthetic effect practically unknown to criticism in the
'nineties. Chopin had resorted to it first of all ; and
at the very time when Hadow wrote the above sentence
it was being further extended by Debussy, to the
intense bewilderment of critics who lacked imagination.

The importance of distinguishing between discursive
intellect and imagination will further appear from the
following instance. Dealing with an unusual chord—
say, for the sake of argument, the one which I invent :

—the devotee of atonality may point out that it consists of three superimposed triads, each in a different key. Another may discover with glee that the fundamentals of these triads may be considered as three notes belonging to the dominant seventh of the key of E, viz. D sharp (for E flat), A, and B. And a third analyst may dismiss these descriptions with the remark that the chord is to be conceived as a minor ninth with various enharmonics and appoggiaturas, thus :

As a single chord, simple or complicated, is analysed, so may a passage be, or the tonal plan of a whole work. Elsewhere, the analyst will tell us that a motive is the inversion, augmented and with additional passing notes, of the second fragment of a theme previously heard ; or that the form of a movement is that of a modified Rondo whose refrain, bi-thematic, provides materials used at certain spots within the couplets.

Thus to find definitions for the features of a work is a process which cannot serve as a foundation for criticism ; it will never show whether the things labelled constitute evidence of artistic interest and logic or not. The significance of a chord in a musical scheme resides not in the notes it consists of but in its functions, in the part it plays within the scheme. No theory makes this principle clearer than Hugo Riemann's, despite its shortcomings in other respects. Every chord in a tonal scheme, he tells us (*Handbuch*

68

der Harmonielehre), has a function which remains in direct relation with the three main functions, tonic, dominant, and subdominant. This function is not necessarily determined, he adds, by the actual notes of which the chord consists. Hence it appears that when we label a certain triad ' tonic ', it is only a short way of expressing its function as a centre, a starting-point, a point of repose, a goal. It is the feeling which it conveys, in itself and apart from any question of labelling, that matters. Likewise, a discord is not a certain combination of notes, but a contrast, a perturbation, an element of motion. Such things should be felt, not puzzled out.

There is a method of harmonic analysis (illustrated in the imaginary example above) which deals with chords as if they were a message in cipher. But even in code-picking, it is not the relationship between the disguised symbols and the actual symbols which will help the would-be reader : it is the relationships between the disguised symbols, without further reference. In letter-codes, and to a great extent in word-codes, it is possible to see almost at once that the relationships between units in cipher are exactly what they are between units in clear. Where analysis and statistics fall short, it is imagination that provides the solution.

The aesthetic value of form resides solely in the reciprocal relationship of parts within a whole, exactly as, in the matter of harmony, the question is what things are, not what it is possible to call them. Where a sense of natural, inner relationship is needed, labelling the parts will supply merely an artificial, outer substitute. If we admit that unity and logic in form depend solely upon the presence of certain correspondences or contrasts, which in works of past periods stand out as tangible symbols of certain types of unity and logic, we may eventually reach a stage when we shall be incapable of seeing further. People who see in the presence of such symbols a proof that the unity of a work is merely formal are no less misled by appearances, labels.

In short, it is suggested that no adequate critical conclusions can be derived from the data of music, the mind alone being powerless to establish standards of judgement. If these propositions are admitted, it may become far easier to consider the facts of music to useful purpose, and to discover the confirmatory proofs and satisfactory explanations which they sometimes afford.

CHAPTER V

INDIRECT DATA AND STANDARDS

I

'Who has solved the riddle of Beethoven's last
'quartets and sonatas? Their interpretation must
'rest upon a sympathetic study of the composer's
'emotional life at the time when they were conceived.
'Tell us what Beethoven suffered or dreamed when
'he wrote any of these works, and you will offer us
'the key to his meaning.' Thus did Ambros formulate
a principle of musical exegesis whose literary prototype
is to be found in the work of Sainte-Beuve.

Sainte-Beuve declared that he found it impossible
to judge a work without knowing all about the man
who wrote it. Taine is equally concerned with seeing
the man in his work; but, as he explains in the
Preface to his *History of British Literature*, his method
is to start from the works and thence, by a dialectic
process of analysis and synthesis, to determine the
author's physical and mental features. Hennequin, in
La Critique scientifique (Paris, 1888), posits that 'it
'is in the works only that the analyst must seek the
'data which will serve to determine their authors'
'individuality'. And Romain Rolland (*Histoire de
l'Opéra en Europe avant Lulli et Scarlatti*, Paris, p. 9)
writes: 'A few pages of a great composer's music
'will tell us more about his soul than his biographies
'or his correspondence.'

It is between these two conceptions of the critic's
attitude towards biographical information that the
student must make up his mind—apart from deciding
for himself whether the well-worn idea of 'seeing the

71

man in his music' means anything more than being conscious of his imaginative idiosyncrasies and artistic aims.

Even in the matter of literature there is a good deal to be said against Sainte-Beuve's principle. If a work does not afford signs pointing to its author's idiosyncrasies with unmistakable significance, the least danger is that the critic may be led to interpret in the light of outside evidence such signs as he discovers, without asking himself searchingly enough whether his interpretation is justified; he may find things which may be considered as signs, and consider them as such merely on the strength of his expectations. In short, he may be led to do exactly the reverse of what we are justified in expecting from him : to become uncritical. In musical criticism, the danger is far greater than ever, since the medium of music does not provide a check and a corrective as definite as the medium of literature.

Indirect data are of two kinds : they may occur in the author's biography and letters, and refer to his disposition, his ideals, the events of his life, and so on ; or they may consist of his statement of what his intentions were in composing a work, or whence he derived the impulse that led him to compose it— i. e. constitute a positive clue to the work's trend, meaning, or *raison d'être*. This second kind of data may be vague, as with a mere title like Smetana's *Aus meinem Leben*, or definite only so far as it specifies the mood and general trend of a work, as with the titles of Liszt's *Festklänge* and *Héroïde funèbre*, of Debussy's *Prélude à l'Après-midi d'un Faune* (naturally, titles such as Dvořák's ' New World ' symphony, indicating merely the origin of its themes, do not come under this heading). Something of the plan and gradation may be revealed, as by the title of the first movement in Debussy's *La Mer: De l'Aube à Midi sur la Mer*. Or the composer having derived the plan and tone of a work from a ' programme ' may publish

72

this programme in full or in brief. Sometimes a title may suggest that the plan of a work was determined by a programme, either because it refers us to a well-known poetic subject, like *Hamlet* or *L'Apprenti Sorcier*, or because it shows that the work embodies some special intention (usually symbolic or philosophical)—as with Scriabin's *Le Divin Poème* and Strauss's *Also sprach Zarathustra*.

2

The question how far the relations between a work and its 'programme' may affect appraisement is important enough to call for the student's utmost attention. The reply to it is so very much a matter of personal feeling, of personal trend of mind and imagination, that it may be wiser to refrain from even the slightest hint on the matter. But it may be useful to set forth the various aspects of the problem, and the solutions so far offered.

One reply is that music, being a self-contained art, 'which aims at representing nought but that which it is in itself' (Hugo Riemann), has nothing to gain and much to lose by being related with, and even by originating in, a programme.

Another is that as soon as music expresses anything, and thereby ceases to be merely formal, it is to be studied as programme music (F. Niecks, *Programme Music in the last Four Centuries*). This is a way of solving the problem by ignoring its actual terms, the result being that the problem is merely shifted.

A third is that programme music, when acceptable from the purely musical point of view (nobody denies that it may be acceptable, if only occasionally), may acquire an additional interest from its relation to an interesting programme. This is the line taken by Ernest Newman (*Musical Studies*).

These three solutions take it for granted that programme music is listened to as one thing and pure music as another. The opinion that programme music and pure music should be listened to exactly in the same spirit; that there is plenty of programme music which can be listened to exactly as a Bach Toccata or a Mozart Quartet, and that the primary test is the possibility of enjoying it exactly as pure music is enjoyed, has also been put forward (see the present writer's 'Esquisse d'une Esthétique de la Musique à Programme', *Sammelbände der Internationalen Musik-Gesellschaft*, ix. 3, pp. 424 sq.; *Musical Times*, 1913, pp. 371 and 439).

The choice between possible replies depends, to a degree, upon each critic's reply to the following questions: Does music suggest emotions, or is it an object of emotion? Admitting that picturesque, poetic, dramatic data, or even purely abstract ideas, suggest to composers certain rhythms, colours, patterns, and structural schemes, does the resulting music prove capable of suggesting these starting-points to listeners by a converse process? Is this the desired result? Is it a desirable result? If so, should not a line be drawn somewhere?

The student will have to decide whether any one of this last batch of questions may receive a reply of principle, or whether the reply to each should vary according to circumstances. In the case of purely emotional data, joyous or tragic, exhilarating or depressing, of pure moods, little doubt appears to exist; and it is generally agreed that the programme simply determines a special order, an unusual form, or deflexions within the range of acknowledged forms. This brings us back to the problem: how is satisfactory form discernible from unsatisfactory form? In the case of direct, physical imitation (splash of water, tramp of footsteps, &c.), the doubt is hardly greater, but the aesthetic value of the association is generally accepted as nil. Yet, whereas some people incline to overlook it, with others, it outweighs all

74

considerations, and any effect which may be classed as imitative is deemed worthy of contempt.

There is even greater disagreement when the connexion between a theme and its poetic or cognitive *primum mobile* is the outcome of an abstract association. This occurs when a certain mood or notion of any kind having suggested a pattern, the opposite mood or notion suggests the same pattern inverted—an occurrence of which examples are to be found even in contemporary music. It is sometimes alleged that even an ascending or descending progression can only be referred to the physical notion of ascent or descent by virtue of verbal association.

Now the inversion of a theme, or an ascending or descending sequence of notes, may have a musical value apart from any question of association. This may be equally true of anything which associations or imitative or descriptive intentions may suggest, or perhaps of certain things only. Hence the need to decide whether the various questions considered above do not reduce themselves in the last instance to these two : is it possible for any kind of associative significance to compensate for any inadequacy in the purely musical significance? And is it possible that where a doubt exists, knowledge of the composer's incentive or purpose may throw light on the question of his actual achievement, not on that of his intentions only?

No reply is possible without regard to each listener's disposition. It may be tempting, it may be reasonable to agree that the highest type of listener is the type to whom music suggests the fewest associations. But there are quantities (probably a large majority) of people to whom music, even of the most ' abstract ' type, is constantly suggesting definite feelings or concrete images. They are—at least part of them—very different from the ' purely emotional listener ' referred to in the passage quoted on p. 51 above, and also from the people to whom music is a field for the mind only.

They may be, in fact, highly imaginative, and not at all slaves of the influence of these associations or suggestions. They may be perfectly justified in asserting that they never fail to pay due attention to the purely musical value of whatever they listen to, although finding additional interest or pleasure in associations. To determine exactly where 'purely musical significance' begins and ends, either for them or in a general meaning, may prove as difficult a task in the case of poetic or programme music as in any other.

All that can be done is once again to warn the student against the danger of allowing for the composer's intentions when considering his achievements.

If we agree that to do so, even when a composer seems to be asking us to, may spell disaster, it will become obvious that the critic is justified in looking askance at evidence which points, not to a composer's professed purpose, but to his possible purpose. It may be true or not that some actual definite mood, determinable by reference to the facts of his biography, prompted him to write a work, or to write it in a certain spirit. He may have yielded to this mood or reacted against it. Thus are we told (perhaps quite rightly) by various biographers of Beethoven that certain works express melancholy moods of his, and other works show him seeking solace in an ideal world of exhilaration. The only thing that matters is whether these works are characteristic and satisfying : the reply lies in the music. Everything else is of anecdotic, not critical, value. There is no reason to hold anecdote in contempt, and we all know that it is a genuinely valuable auxiliary during the kindergarten stages of education.

3

But it may occur that biographical facts are inaccurate. One signal instance is at hand, embodying a lesson which can hardly be ignored.

76

If there is one thing on which all agree, it is that music should originate in creative imagination at white heat. The fact that a composer wrote a certain work at great speed, or in a frenzy of excitement, may not be a sufficient proof of 'white heat', but may be admitted as a collateral proof, exactly as any other piece of biographical evidence might be. Berlioz, in his 'Memoirs' and elsewhere, tells us that this work of his was written in a few hours; that when engaged in writing this other, ideas poured in so rapidly that he had to devise 'a special kind of shorthand' to note them down, and so on. The 'Marche au Supplice' in the *Symphonie fantastique* was written 'during a night of fever' of which he spent the greater part roving through snow-clad fields while Chopin and Liszt sought his corpse at the Paris mortuary. The 'night of fever' part of the statement was accepted by his biographers and critics until the day when one of them, Adolphe Boschot, examined the autograph manuscript of the March and found it to be part of the score of his opera *Les Francs-Juges*, inserted into the score of the *Symphonie fantastique* without any further alteration than the addition of four bars written on a piece of staved paper affixed by wafers (Boschot, *La Jeunesse d'un Romantique*, Paris, 1906, pp. 394 and 421).

This affects the question of the March's interest and fitness as little as the 'night of fever' story affects it the other way. We know that many composers have transferred music bodily from one work to another. There must be countless instances which we shall never know. Even this March, in its original form, may have been written as Berlioz would have us believe it was. But the value of the collateral evidence to that effect is obviously nil.

Chamfort relates that the court-painter Coypel, when about to exhibit side by side his original portrait of the Duc de Bourgogne and a replica he had made of it, was asked by Louis XIV : ' Tell me on which ' side the original will be : for it would be unsuitable ' for me to go wrong.'

Unfortunately, circumstantial evidence appears to carry more weight—so far as current examples of criticism may serve as proofs—than the internal evidence. Of what value can the indirect evidence provided by the existence of an original be to a critic judging a copy?

It is, assuredly, of great importance so far as his preliminary education is concerned. Exactly as the only way to acquire a fine sense of musical beauty is to compare admittedly good music with admittedly bad (which will not mean that these two labels are not subject to revision), so is it particularly instructive to compare a work which we consider original—or are told is original—with an imitation of it, supposed or real.

It is useful, again, when describing a work as an imitation, to clinch the argument by referring to its model. But to say ' This work is unoriginal. If you doubt it, compare it with this other ' is one thing, and to decide that a work is unoriginal on the mere strength of the fact that we are acquainted with the model, another. The critic should be capable of knowing genuineness from imposture without outside help.

Friedrich Wilhelm Rust (1739–96) was described as a composer of prophetic genius, whose music in many respects anticipated Beethoven's. Not only Dr. Prieger, but experts such as Vincent d'Indy and Paul Dukas accepted the published versions as a matter of course (d'Indy, however, wrote in the second volume of his *Treatise of Composition*, p. 219, that the published text contained a few objectionable but otherwise unimportant alterations). One is glad to remember that others, such as John Shedlock (*The Pianoforte Sonata*, 1895, pp. 152 sq.), remained sceptical. Eventually, it turned out that Rust's grandson, Dr. Wilhelm Rust, had garbled the texts, introducing in them precisely the passages which had been singled out by critics as specially prophetic. (On this matter, see articles in the *Musical Times*, January and April 1913.)

Of course, it is quite possible in principle for a composer to turn a formless sketch by another composer into a masterpiece. Or he may deal with an imperfect work and alter it for the best without impairing its character and merits. This, we are sometimes told, is what Rimsky-Korsakof did with Mussorgsky's *Boris Godunof*. I have often wondered whether anybody could determine the extent and bearing of Rimsky-Korsakof's alterations except by comparing the genuine text with the altered. It is quite possible, anyhow, to conceive instances when it would be impossible to determine anything of the kind. It is all a matter of tact, sense of fitness, and so forth. In other words, the arranger must be an artist and capable of doing exactly what the original author might have thought fit to do. Further than that we cannot go, nor is it needful for our present purposes to raise any other question. Granting for the sake of argument that there is no reason of principle why alterations should always be objectionable, and critics always capable of discerning them, it remains true that in such matters the critic should not be at the mercy of indirect evidence. And to put any degree of trust in indirect evidence of any kind is to place oneself altogether at its mercy.

Let it be made clear that indirect evidence may settle the question whether a work (say Beethoven's recently-discovered *Jena Symphony*) is by a certain composer or not. This is not what should interest the critic who aims at an aesthetic valuation. Composer's names, after all, are but labels, indirect evidence, which may sway our judgement one way or the other. Critics are often accused (not always without grounds) of being influenced by considerations of the composer's name, age, nationality, school, and even sex. No one can finally disprove an accusation of this kind, but every one should and can make sure that he will never act so as to deserve it.

Evidence to the effect that a symphony was written by Beethoven, or by an unknown contemporary of his, or by a twentieth-century composer whose style and methods resemble Beethoven's, is about as useful for purposes of appraisement as evidence to the effect that ' Homer's works were not written by him but by somebody else bearing the same name '.

5

There is one kind of indirect evidence, however, for which a special case may be made. If we have heard half a dozen works by a composer and liked or disliked them, it may influence our attitude towards the next work of his we hear. Clearly the only form which this influence may legitimately take is that of a warning to devote additional care and scruple to the examination of this next work.

To be acquainted with a composer, to hear him talk of his work, explain his views and purposes, is both useful and dangerous. It may lead us to identify ourselves with him, and accordingly to jeopardize, on the strength of the indirect evidence provided by him, something of our own ability to deal with the internal evidence provided by his achievements.

In short, all indirect data, like the data examined in the previous chapter, are useful only after the event, so far as they bring confirmation. Indirect standards may be even more dangerous than standards originating in natural disposition.

CHAPTER VI

WHAT HISTORY TEACHES THE CRITIC

I

THE parallel courses of evolution of the art of music, of musical taste, and of criticism are most instructive. The first point to appear is that while creative artists were for ever extending their scope, criticism kept protesting in the name of alleged laws—the very laws in whose formation we have been trying to determine the extent of the influence of habit and system.

By way of illustration, a few remarks from various periods are appended.

' Poets are fond of inconsistent mixture ; they make
' further havoc by separating the rhythm and figure
' of the dance from the melody, and the melody and
' rhythm from the words. Where there are no words,
' it is very difficult to recognize the meaning of
' harmony and rhythm . . . this sort of thing which
' aims only at . . . brutish noise is exceedingly rude
' and coarse ; it leads to every kind of irregularity
' and trickery.'

(Plato, *Laws*, Bk. II, Jowett's translation, vol. v, pp. 240–1.)

' How dare they sing or write Discant, those who
' ignore the art of selecting chords, and have no inkling
' which combinations of sounds constitute concords ? '

(Johannes De Muris, fourteenth century.)

' You hear a medley of sounds, a variety of parts,
' a rumble of harmonies that are intolerable to the
' ear. One sings in quick tempo, another in slow ;

F

' one voice has top notes, another deep notes ; and
' as if this was not enough a third remains midway . . .
' with all the best will in the world, how can the mind
' see light in this chaos ? '
(Artusi on Monteverdi, 1608.)

' Three of the movements of Beethoven's symphony
' in A are without any settled design, confused, full
' of harsh combinations.'
(Criticism dated 1823, quoted in the *Musical
Times*, October 1922, p. 733.)

' I examined the autograph manuscript of the work.
' Mozart actually wrote this irregular chord. Let us
' not say, with Haydn, that he had his reasons for
' doing so : errors of this kind offend our reason, our
' senses, and our taste.' (Fétis on Mozart, 1839.)

' An affectation of Beethoven's was to invent new
' forms, not so much under the impulse of inspiration
' as in order to adhere to a preconceived plan.'
(The same writer, 1834.)

' No form, no design, no rhythm, no symmetry.'
(D'Ortigue on Wagner, 1861.)

' I heard sounds in uninterrupted sequence, without
' finding a trace of design, of form, of a motive, of an
' accent.'
(A French writer on Debussy's *Pelléas et
Mélisande*, 1902.)

' The ear is helpless, one feels irritated and bored.'
(Another, on the same topic, 1902.)

' Unmeaning bunches of notes . . . clotted nonsense.'
(F. Corder on Schönberg, *Musical
Quarterly*, 1915.)

' Wild insanities such as intellectualized art disdains
' to touch ; and the spirits of ugliness and destruction
' abolish the final intellectual bondage of euphony

82

'itself. . . . The period of deepest musical degradation
' . . . shamelessly avowed in cretinous babble by
' Schönberg and Stravinsky.'
(Rutland Boughton, *Musical Times*, 1922.)

It is sometimes alleged that quotations of this kind
prove nothing. Thus Ernest Newman writes (*Sunday
Times*, 19 November 1922) :

'Why do historians go on repeating one after
' another the false judgement of some contemporary
' critic or other, instead of trying to find out what
' the mass of plain sensible hearers thought of the new
' work? If historians would only take that trouble,
' they would find that nine great works out of ten have
' been seen from the commencement to be great.'

But it is enough if they show the need for the
critic to concentrate his energies upon proving as
capable of discerning good from bad as the ' plain
sensible hearer ' is, or rather upon aiming at becoming,
in Hadow's words, ' the most enlightened listener '.
They substantiate the fact emphasized by a writer
(quoted by Newman, ibid., 22 April 1923) who
contrasted the attitude of the untutored man at a
performance of a new work with that of the trained
musician. The former, he said, ' is able, without an
' effort, to listen objectively to what he hears, and
' judge it for what it is worth ; whilst the professionally
' trained musician is subconsciously collating his im-
' pressions with the technique which, as it was imparted
' to him in musical infancy, has become to him sacro-
' sanct. In other words, he has a difficulty in hearing
' music as it sounds, without at the same time hearing
' how it ought to sound according to his conception
' of music. Metaphorically he is listening with a blue
' pencil, though he may be unaware of the fact.'

Stripped of all but essentials, these quotations (and
hundreds of others which are to be encountered every

F 2

day) reduce themselves to three statements : the music heard tried the ear, ran contrary to the hearers' customs or tenets, and did not make sense for them. The identity of ideas and the resemblances in wording leave no room for doubt. Of course, no sensible human being would think that the fact that protest against a contemporary composer's music runs on the same lines as protest previously uttered against works which have since proved great is one to build upon for controversial purposes : it may, however, be used as a reminder.

2

With regard to the ' mass of plain sensible hearers ', there is in Arnold Bennett's *Literary Taste and How to Form It* a remark which will help us to dispose of the fallacy—lurking behind those five words—that new music is best judged by the average public :

' The fame of classical authors is entirely indepen-
' dent of the majority. It is originally made, and it
' is maintained, by a passionate few. Even when
' a first-class author has enjoyed immense success
' during his lifetime, the majority have never appre-
' ciated him so sincerely as they have appreciated
' second-rate men. In the case of an author who has
' emerged into glory after his death the happy sequel
' has been due solely to the obstinate perseverance of
' the few. They kept on savouring him and talking
' about him, and generally behaved with such eager
' zeal that at last the majority placidly agreed that he
' was a genius.'

These passionate few, in music, are the ' most enlightened listeners '. Not all are so enlightened as to admire fully and adequately from the outset, in the works they admire, precisely the qualities which later will prove most admirable. Nor is their verdict necessarily endorsed at the outset, or even known to the public at large. For a time, judgements clash with one another. The importance of any individual judgement proves in the long run to be exceedingly small. Indeed, it is not so much any individual verdict that matters, as the methods by which it is reached and the balance of elements (possibly conflicting elements) which it represents. It often occurs that a particular objection levelled at a great work when it first appeared, and long forgotten, crops up again in the verdicts representing for the later generations the nearest approach to finality that criticism may hope to effect. But then undue importance is no longer ascribed to this objection. For instance, it is quite possible to-day to agree with certain of the criticisms directed against Wagner's music by his first critics, and yet to reject their estimate of his work as preposterously wrong.

Judgements mature and react upon one another. Hence an eventual adjustment. This adjustment may strike an average between extremes; but, as a rule, this will occur only with regard to works whose significance is not above the average. Really significant works seem fated to arouse forthwith great enthusiasm and great indignation, except in the not infrequent cases when they pass comparatively unnoticed. But even upon this we cannot build. If we study history carefully, we shall see that when a work is highly praised by some people, bitterly inveighed against by others, it does not mean that truth stands midway any more than it means that the work will eventually emerge victorious. Nor can we be guided by the number or even by the qualifications of the critics who pronounced one way or the other.

3

Currents of taste exist at all periods, with the consequence that a verdict true in the main will be subjected to temporary readjustment. As regards

France, these currents have been admirably studied by Lionel de la Laurencie in his book *Le Goût musical en France*.

Reaction against the immediate past is a characteristic feature of all periods. Indeed, this symptom recurs so uniformly that it is devoid of special significance in any particular case. It often occurs that the transition between periods is marked by an outbreak of purely experimental works, of ventures not justified by achievement. But this, again, provides no rule for the critic's guidance. As a matter of fact, it is only long after the event that we see whether a given period was essentially transitional or not. And the possibility that works of enduring beauty may crop up even in the midst of such a period is not negligible.

In short, there is nothing in the teachings of history to make us feel confident in the safety of generalizing, except on certain points which provide warnings rather than positive help. We know, for instance, that a very small proportion of the music written survives the test of time, and that the fact that music conformed to the particular requirements of a period is no guarantee of survival. We know what the requirements of the passionate few, the most enlightened listeners, must for ever be ; and also that it is impossible to formulate them except in terms so general that they constitute no practical standard for the critic. We see that as a rule the precept holds good in which Sainte-Beuve has subtly expressed the difference between the classic and the academic : ' Il ne faut point paraître classique trop tôt si on veut le demeurer longtemps,' and that the spirit of revolution proves as barren as that of academicism when revolution becomes what academicism is, namely, an end and not a means. We also see, running through the turmoil of action and reaction, a thin but strong thread for our guidance. In Bennett's words, ' the one reassuring affair is that the

86

' passionate few are passionate about the same things '.
We may add with Hennequin (*La Critique scientifique*,
p. 59) : ' Qualitative appreciation of art is, com-
' paratively speaking, a constant quantity. It is very
' seldom that people who are moved by a work disagree
' about the nature and origin of their emotion. Sub-
' jectivity in appreciation affects the degree rather
' than the nature of impressions.'

This is as near a definition of the common measure
of artistic appreciation as we may, for the time being,
hope to achieve.

4

——It seems almost futile to point out that the critic
must have a thorough knowledge of history and of all
facts relating to the conditions under which the works
he deals with were written. But this may help him
little so far as his main object is concerned. For
instance, anybody not capable of acknowledging the
subtle variety of Haydn's music will profit little by
having his attention called to the fact that time and
circumstances made it imperative for Haydn to conform to certain outward conditions. The wonder is
what Haydn did within the terms of his problem,
quite apart from any question why these terms were
what they were. And if he can feel no difference
between a work by Haydn and a work by one of his
academic imitators, the knowledge that one was
written in the eighteenth century and the other in
the nineteenth will be of little service to him. Study
of conditions, social, technical, and others, properly
belongs to the preliminary education of the critic.
Where knowledge falls short, all kinds of mistakes
occur, as when a critic alleges that a work contains
imitations of another work written years later.

In controversy, accurate and thorough knowledge
may provide valuable arguments. It is sometimes
said that innovators ' destroy the very fundaments

of musical art '. Against such statements it may be useful to show how the practice of innovators may be traced back : Debussy's, for example, through Chabrier's, Mussorgsky's, and Liszt's, as far as Chopin, whose artistic filiation in turn is not beyond reach of investigation. To resort to proofs of this kind is not to accept the notion that ' a thing cannot be good unless it has been done before ' ; nor is it always possible to resort to them usefully. At present attempts are being made to trace the origin of polytonal writing back to Beethoven and even to Bach (by Milhaud—in the *Revue Musicale*, February 1923— among others). They are not very convincing ; and it may be doubted whether for the purposes of criticism they are needful in principle, any more than attempts to connect Debussy with Chopin or Wagner with Weber and Liszt may be, however justified they are from the point of view of the student of artistic evolution.

PART II
THE PRACTICE

CHAPTER I

A RECONSTRUCTION

I

Our quest for common ground providing an acceptable starting-point has not so far been very successful. Again and again we have seen the reasons for agreement on any definite principle dwindle almost to vanishing point; and our budget consists chiefly of indications showing what to avoid or to beware of, and of a modicum of hope derived from the teaching of history. If we are to proceed further, however, it will have to be by virtue of some kind of compromise, of a reconstruction similar to that which Kant gives in his *Kritik der praktischen Vernunft* after the *tabula rasa* of his *Kritik der Reinvernunft*. Otherwise, even if we refuse to admit that musical criticism entirely reduces itself to a matter of opinion, we shall remain unable to show that it does not.

By seeking a compromise, we shall be following for a while the lead of the votaries of criticism by system; for every system is a compromise, an acknowledgement of the impossibility to judge except by reference to a system, to a standard of comparison accessible to the intellect. But this need not deter us : we are in quest of a more satisfactory form of compromise, by virtue of which our course will follow a method and not a system, and which will include reference to no fixed or insufficiently congruous standard. That such a form is possible is shown not only by abstract or general reasons, but by reasons that are actual and specific.

Music is no ideal thing intended for ideal listeners, but a real thing for real listeners. We must not treat it as we might if there were no such things as idiosyncrasies, predispositions, and prejudices. These are part of the critic's problem, and all in the day's work. The Kantian problem, whether our knowledge adjusts itself to its object, or whether the object is merely what our knowledge makes it, is not part of the critic's problem. We have seen that reason may supply no final standard in musical criticism; but it will be enough to satisfy ourselves that it may supply at least a regulating principle.

On this point no doubt exists. We do judge music; we do find reasons in support of our judgements, and even reasons that point straight to the origin of our judgements. At either stage, experience and knowledge tell. Now and then, it is true, they may fail where intuition succeeds. They may lack the power finally to counteract certain of our instincts. But even if the correctives they provide are not all-powerful, they serve a purpose. Given a human being who loves music and wishes to know why he loves it, and why his attitude towards it varies in degree and in kind, experience and knowledge certainly will assist him. They further assist the critic who seeks the right way of inviting others to share his interest in music and to extend their own, if only by warning him of the obstacles in his way. If our investigation has succeeded in discovering possible sources of error, it has accomplished its purpose so far. There remains to find out how the mind may actually co-operate in the positive part of the critical process.

2

Let us consider a number of works which have proved their lasting vitality, and a number of works now discarded as worthless. We shall usually find it possible to disengage features common to all the

92

former, which perhaps will be common to all the latter as well. The more of these we disengage, the easier it becomes to see the differences beyond the resemblances between good works and bad. This is why comparative experience is so needful in criticism, and why the man who is familiar with many kinds of music and many examples of every kind is not only more receptive, but better able to turn to good purpose the contribution of his mind towards appreciation.

But this need not concern us further for the moment. Nor does it matter whether we agree that the works considered are good or bad. The point is merely that the presence of common features illustrates the fact that artists setting out to create a work start by accepting certain general principles as conditions under which that work will materialize. They ask us to accept these conditions. Conditions of some sort are necessary. Clive Bell rightly defines the artistic problem as ' the problem of making a match between ' an emotional experience and a form which has been ' conceived but not yet created. . . . It will serve the ' double purpose of concentrating the artist's energies ' and stimulating his intellect. It will be at once a canal ' and a goad . . . the ideal problem will be the one ' that raises the artist's power most while limiting his ' fancy least ' (*Since Cézanne*, pp. 43–6).

If criticism is to decide how the problem has been solved, obviously it must be cognizant of all the problem's terms. Granting, again, that imagination only will succeed in deciding how far successful the ' matching ' is, it remains true that the mind (and especially the mind disciplined into mistrust of hasty generalizations) is able to determine what the form conceived is (if only by determining what it is not) and often to ascertain its full possibilities. Where creative imagination has forged ahead, the critic's mind works its way, finding facts and analogies whose importance may be more or less decisive. Acceptance of

93

one condition will be found to imply acceptance of several more, to be compatible with acceptance of certain further conditions, but incompatible with the acceptance of others. Even the newest possible conditions (say atonality, or polytonality, or a principle of construction not founded on the repetition and working-out of motives) will probably have something in common with known conditions, since the evolution of art is gradual. So far as they have, their bearing and consequences may be ascertained—sometimes in full, more often with regard only to the case under notice. We may reach a point when we shall be able to say with confidence that a certain new term in the artist's chosen problem (e.g. such as was introduced, some time ago, by the use of the whole-tone scale) is of trifling, or limited, importance ; that it can neither create a new problem nor affect the bearing of known problems. Where this proves impossible, the possibility of affirming the existence in a composer's problem of unknown quantities is in itself of positive value. The mind will then be satisfied with biding its time.

Hadow, in his Essay of 1906 already quoted from, commented upon the idiom of Debussy's *Pelléas et Mélisande* thus :

' Is it possible, we may ask, that this *genre omni-*
' *tonique* should be as fit a vehicle for epic ideas as
' the diatonic scale of Bach and Beethoven ? If so, it
' will in course of time hold the entire field ; . . . if
' not, it will remain for those forms of composition
' which specially depend on delicacy and refinement
' and suggestion, and will leave to a simpler speech
' the direct utterance of more vital truths.'

He acknowledged, first, the existence of unknown quantities in the problem, created by the introduction of omnitonality ; secondly, that these need not be taken into account when judging *Pelléas et Mélisande*,

94

since the expression of epic ideas was not part of Debussy's problem in this work; and thirdly, that it is not by systematically extracting rules from the omnitonal principle that its artistic value may be ascertained. Compare his procedure with the procedure exemplified by the quotation from Dr. Felber on p. 62 above, and notice the difference in spirit.

Again (*Musical Quarterly*, January 1915), he wrote that Schönberg's piano pieces Op. 11 and 19 'gave 'him the impression that they meant something to 'which he had not yet the clue'. This was several years after various writers had started describing the piece Op. 11 as mere nonsense, without giving any reason except the customary one that it 'did not make sense', nor showing by which process they had reached this conclusion. Apart from any question whether they were, or will eventually be found, right, there can be no doubt that Hadow's attitude was unimpeachable, and theirs very unsatisfactory. Sometimes great moral courage is needed to maintain an attitude of doubt when many people around are shouting 'Hail the discoverer of the promised land!' or 'Down with the impostor!' as the case may be. It is each critic's business to make sure that when he does so, he has good reasons, and is not merely shirking the issue.

3

The main thing is and always remains that whether we pronounce upon the value of the artist's problem or upon the value of his solution, we must make it clear to ourselves (and to our readers so far as is necessary, that is, so far as a new problem is being dealt with) that we are fully aware of this problem's conditions. This is all that is meant by the often misapplied adage that 'we must learn to see things from the composer's point of view'.

There is a thing generally defined as classical harmonic music, whose boundaries are usually described as established by the practice of masters from Bach to Brahms. We know exactly, by experience as well as by theory, how far it can be extended and varied up to the limit when the conceptions of both tonal balance and part-writing which differentiate it from all other possible or imaginable conceptions of music cease to exist. If, then, a writer asserts that ' Brahms ' often evinces indifference towards key-relationship, ' and therefore many of his works lack clarity and ' interest ' (d'Indy, *Cours de Composition musicale*, ii, p. 415), there can be no doubt that he is meeting Brahms on his own ground ; for we know that key-relationship is very decidedly included in Brahms's problem. The statement deserves far greater consideration than the statement that Schönberg in his Op. 11 (or in any other) ignores the importance of key-relationship, unless it be shown that key-relationship is part of Schönberg's problem or a necessary part of all composers' problems. So far the mind proves of help. When it comes to deciding between d'Indy's view and Hadow's, that in Brahms's music ' the choice of keys is always justified by the event ' (*Studies in Modern Music*, ii, p. 290), further discussion is not excluded, although the odds are that it will not lead very far, and that it is imagination which will have the last say ; and this proves at least that much ground has been cleared. The assertion that Schönberg, for instance, evinces indifference towards key-relationship is of no critical value. It clears no ground.

Another simple example will show that as great a quantity of ground may be cleared by the mind even in new problems. There is the whole-tone scale, whose appearance provided at first new elements and extensions in the tonal principle, and later a non-tonal principle of working out and even of actual structure (e.g. in Debussy's *Cloches à travers les feuilles*).

96

In the latter case the mind may struggle to interpret this scale as tonal by accepting, say,

as

and admitting that the sixth note, A sharp or B flat, may do duty for B as well as for A, and so on (a good many people do so instinctively). Or it may resort to considering that the augmented fifth chords which generate the whole-tone scale are peculiar formations whose fundamental note is the middle note (this is Dr. Riemann's point of view), and then feel that the unknown quantity is determined. It may also seek a solution elsewhere.

Let us start by admitting that the whole-tone scale is exactly what it may seem to be, viz. a scale which determines no particular centre for the simple reason that it consists of exactly equidistant intervals. If it does determine a centre our problem is even simpler, but we grant that the composer may treat the scale as if it did not, and select a centre arbitrarily—a right which we shall find ourselves bound to grant when more complex forms of atonal writing confront us.

We accept his problem exactly as he asks us to. We do not start by deciding that the centre must be a tonic characterized by a triad, and further by a subdominant and a dominant with their triads, obvious or disguised, and so on. All we expect from him is that he will give us some kind of order of which the general formula is expressed by the terms

G

' variety in unity ', and which is the most elementary condition of artistic interest.

However, we are justified in pointing out that in the whole-tone scale (under its two possible forms, at a semitone's distance from one another) the possible relations lack both pregnancy and variety ; and that for this very reason the non-tonal use of the scale will not create a complex new problem, nor its use within the tonal scheme a disturbing feature. When Dargomyjsky, in his *Stone-Guest*, wrote the first example of systematic and protracted use of this scale, it was easy to see then and there that it provided a limited range of new resources. In tonal writing, these are a couple of pigments which naturally fell into place among the stock already available (Liszt and Wagner had already seen to that) ; a scale in which practically every pattern possible in the diatonic scale could be duplicated ; and a small number of harmonic elements, neutral so far as tonal function is concerned, and therefore amenable to chromatic treatment, and favourable only to enharmonic modulation and to boundless, methodically erratic sequences very much in the same fashion as diminished sevenths. In nontonal writing the scale provides practically nothing but a kind of see-saw. Sequences of whole-tone chords and of diminished sevenths are meaningless except as colour-effects or by reference to a tonal scheme in which they appear. This obvious point shows that even certain processes (here that of the sequence) imply the acceptance of certain conditions : sequences imply, if not the actual conditions of tonality, then the conditions of some scheme as definite in range and in sharp differentiations as the usual tonal scheme is, so as to determine the functions of sequences within it.

Many such signs may be noticed in new and more complex formations such as arise from the use of the chords in fourths which have lately come into pro-

98

minence. As described in Schönberg's *Harmonielehre* (1st ed., pp. 446 sq.) they show practically boundless and definite possibilities of articulation. They may co-operate with the usual chords in the usual tonal scheme, or provide the foundation of schemes in which nothing subsists of the relationships constituting the tonal scheme. Even then, and in every conceivable way of writing music, the elementary conditions of order and unity and variety will have to be observed in some fashion, which must have some points in common with the fashions we are familiar with.

Nor is the problem of polytonality complicated. It is really simpler than the problems of atonal writing. For the critic's mind it amounts very much to the same thing as playing several games concurrently for the chess player's; the additional question of the aesthetic significance of the whole concerns not his mind but his imagination. There is also a question of ear-training, or, rather, one of the ear's endurance. If eventually the physical displeasure caused by the clash of polytonal combinations proves such that only an effort of mind and of will-power enables a listener to endure it, for that listener, be he a critic or not, the problem is solved. The fact that combinations which were intolerable a few decades ago are nowadays found quite pleasurable does not imply that there is no limit to the ear's tolerance. And if it turns out that polytonal music is not meant for the ear and does not stimulate the imagination, polytonal music will have to go.

Thus do we learn from the experience which adjustment to the conditions of tonal writing has provided us with to adjust ourselves to the new conditions— not necessarily in order to accept them, but in order to have a clear perception of them. If this obvious and most useful teaching of previous experience is often disregarded (especially in current books on Musical Appreciation), it is partly because the process of adjustment to the conditions of tonal music is so easy with us (as well it may be considering that we are born and live surrounded in an atmosphere of tonal music) as to pass unnoticed, and partly because the principles of tonal music are often considered to be the natural outcome of a universal law of music. But even if they are, we have to imbibe them gradually. And when we read the books in which they are explained, we see that they are not so simple an affair after all.

Once the adjustment to new conditions is effected, our mind will begin to see light. In proportion as the way in which the composers use the new resources compares with the way in which others have used the old, the unknown quantities in their problems become fewer and easier to deal with. For instance, in their works there must be passages serving as links or transitions. Our experience will enable us to detect them as such, and then we shall be able to compare them with the passages that are not. Failing these, there will be progressions, climaxes, contrasts, points of movement and points of repose, or something else to lay hands on. We shall gradually acquire a sense of the provisionally indefinable logic of a composer's style, in which things such as a *de facto* reversal to processes excluded, or restricted in significance, by the essential conditions of his problem (as sequences in whole-tone writing and consecutive fifths in usual tonal part-writing) will sound as unmistakably incongruous as an equivalent antinomy in any other scheme : it may be the use of tonal motives within a non-tonal scheme in which the essential properties of such motives are disregarded ; or repetition (perhaps disguised) *ad nauseam*, or a vicious circle such as diminished sevenths or augmented fifths create elsewhere ; it may be a thousand different, hitherto unsuspected things. So far as they occur, they help us to ascertain how the composer is handling his problem, our mind co-operating with our emotions and imagination.

CHAPTER II

FORMING JUDGEMENTS

I

So long as emotions, mind, and imagination agree, the difficulties of criticism are reduced to a minimum. It is when a conflict arises that trouble begins. It may also have occurred, without our being aware of it, that either the mind or the imagination has failed to take part in the critical operation. This is inexpedient. A judgement emanating from the mind alone may crop up easily and be sound so far as it goes; but it will probably not go very far. A judgement formed by the imagination alone will perhaps crop up even more easily, and probably be more far-reaching; but it remains unchecked, and in criticism has no value beyond that of a toss. If mind and imagination work jointly, the process will often be slower and more difficult. Exactly as two beams of light thrown together under certain conditions produce not a better illumination but the phenomenon known as interference, so will perplexities now and then occur. An adjustment may follow, or one faculty will get the upper hand. Referring to Stendhal's assertion that Rossini, in the Darkness scene in *Mosé*, displayed ' science in conjunction with an abundance of ideas ', Lionel de la Laurencie (*Le Goût musical en France*, p. 13) points out that the music of this scene consists solely of twenty-six repetitions of one pattern. Here it is clear enough that the mind's contribution may outweigh that of the imagination which sees ' abundance of ideas ' in a passage comprising only one idea, and science in mere repetition.

A similar case was made more than once against Wagner's prelude to *Rheingold*. But the writers who adduced as evidence of its alleged monotony that it consisted of 136 bars without one change in harmony, and of one motive only, did not state the case in full. There is plenty of science in Wagner's handling of his materials, and he shows no lack of the very ideas which could best ensure the achievement of his object, namely, a long and telling gradation. If a critic could point to something similar in the *Mosé* scene, La Laurencie's statement would cease to be of value. But even though the mind, by analysing the *Rheingold* Prelude, can make more than a fair case in its favour, the reason why most people agree to consider it as inspired, and not as the mechanical carrying out of a plan not particularly interesting in itself, is that it appeals to their imagination.

2

In a previous chapter I spoke of rules reaching the recipe stage. This may refer to composers who write mechanically, by rule-of-thumb, and to critics who judge no less mechanically.) It is essential that the critic should discover some means of detecting rule-of-thumb music. The one form of criticism which will always remain powerless to do this is rule-of-thumb criticism, which adopts a recipe as its standard.) The recipe may be ' good music should follow the usual rules ', or it may be ' good music should break them '. It makes no difference. In one case rule-of-thumb criticism will prove incapable of dealing with works that do not conform with the recipe and of discriminating between works that do ; in the other, it will assume that the breaking is all that matters, and fail to detect methods of breaking which may be as mechanical as the most mechanical obedience.)

The possible existence of signs pointing to mechanical writing is of greater importance to-day than it has ever been since the question of method in musical criticism first arose, because of the surprising rapidity with which composers of all schools have started casting aside principles or conventions. The position is no longer quite what it was when the differences between original creations and mechanical products were few and perhaps restricted to points of detail.

In the particular case of scales, the right to adopt or to create scales is now claimed by many composers, of whom some, mayhap, exercise this right by dint of sheer mechanical ingenuity. Scriabin elected frequently to use a special scale (elaborately described in a number of books and notices dealing with him). Whether this scale was mechanically contrived may remain debatable ; but there can be no question that a composer may appear any day who, by the simple device of using semitones where Scriabin uses wholetones and vice versa, will present us with an alleged brand-new scale and ensuing system of chord-building, both mechanically devised. He may be doing so without having deliberately set out to deceive us ; he may be deceiving himself. He may have thought that a certain process would suit his genuinely conceived purpose, and resorted to it in all good faith. It is the issue alone that we have to judge.

Unavoidably his contrivance will be the outcome of a distortion or combination of some thing or things already known. To this there is no alternative. It is as sure as it is sure that nobody can contrive an image, however novel and fantastic, of animal or plant or banshee, except out of elements already known. But if his methods are very clever and thorough, the critic will certainly have his work cut out. (Often the passing of judgement will have to be left to imagination, and belief in it to faith.) But elsewhere it is possible to discover signs of distortion or of equivalent processes.) A few years ago, a notice of a new symphony included the following statement : ' The scherzo is in

103

' 5-8 time. But the rhythm is halting and leaves one
' with the impression that a beat has been knocked
' out of a pattern whose natural rhythm would be in
' 6-8 time, the composer being guided by his desire
' to write at all costs his scherzo in 5-8.'

Here we have an alleged fact (halting rhythm), the
implication that the motive as it stands suggests a
6–8 metre, and the judgement that the scherzo is
a laboured product, not the outcome of spontaneous
creative imagination. The value of the criticism
depends upon the critic's capacity to decide where
natural rhythm ends and halting rhythm begins.) The
fact and the implication together create at least the
appearance that a fair case is made. Had the writer
completed it by quoting the pattern he refers to, he
would have done all that a critic can be expected to
do. But the impression of finality conveyed is so
manifest, that unless his statement is true the criticism
is most unfair.

3

This kind of evidence is not always easily found, nor
trustworthy. Many attempts are made to show on
similar grounds that certain strange things in modern
music can be reduced to the veriest commonplaces.
This will not necessarily mean that they were derived
from these commonplaces by distortion, nor, of course,
that their value is merely that of the commonplace
plus or minus the value of the distorting process.
Malipiero, in his pamphlet *Orchestration*, resorts to
the argument with regard to examples of Schönberg's music. When capital is made out of discoveries
of that sort, they are bound to be fairly obvious and
simple. If far-fetched, they would hardly appear
convincing even if they corresponded to facts. And
needless to say that if an analysis of a piece on these
lines is to be conclusive—even from the point of view
of the mind alone—it must cover the whole ground :

form and courses of procedure as well as character of motives and other materials. The analysis of the materials alone will not be enough without additional evidence at least to the effect that there is no trace of originality in the way in which they are used. And the mind is apt to behave strangely with regard to cumulative evidence in matters of music. A critic may adduce substantial reasons for his view that (*a*) the materials, (*b*) the working out, (*c*) the form, and (*d*) the instrumental writing of a work consist of commonplaces, disguised or not, and are mechanically devised : and somebody else may be prepared to grant these assertions one after the other, and yet challenge the conclusion that the work as a whole is commonplace and uninteresting. As likely as not his argument will be some variant of the old (and quite sound) adage that a work of art is the product, not merely the sum, of its parts ; he will contend that there are subtle spiritual elements which should not be overlooked. The reply may be that in arithmetic, when the parts are sufficiently few and small, their product may be no greater than their sum, or even smaller (e. g. $1 \cdot 5 \times 1 \cdot 5 < 1 \cdot 5 + 1 \cdot 5$). One critic will be alleging that the several parts of the work under discussion are paltry, and poorly put together, the other will be alleging the reverse. It amounts to one saying that his imagination is not fired, and the other saying that his is : a deadlock is reached. It is neither by similes nor by pitting affirmation against affirmation that problems of criticism can be solved.

4

The difficulty of recognizing commonplaces and mechanical devices is not proportionate with the number of elements to be considered nor with the complication of disguises—provided the imagination has given a clue. But perhaps the difficulty of proving the point so as to compel other people to acknowledge it is. Musical criticism has not reached a stage when equal importance will be ascribed to originality in treatment and originality in choice of materials. Indeed, the reverse is often implied, much being made of the fact that composers have borrowed themes or passages, but the question whether they resort or not to unoriginal methods of treatment and structure being seldom mentioned, if ever. The sole egregious exceptions, in fact, are the reverse of what it would be natural to expect. It is not composers who adhere to the usual conventions that are accused of being unoriginal in their methods, but composers who tread newly-opened paths. The reason, of course, is that every new departure in music—quite apart from the possible variety of application it may lend itself to—is for a time considered as something exceptional. Criticism, then, takes a form such as ' a composer who uses leitmotives is an imitator of Wagner ', or ' a composer who uses certain harmonies and colour-effects is an imitator of Debussy '.

It is interesting to note that whereas Hadow lays stress upon what he terms ' the principle of vitality ', namely, ' the composer should be the parent of his ideas and not their fabricator ' (*Studies in Modern Music*, i, p. 15), he does not say that this principle should apply to treatment as well. In fact, he says that it applies ' so far as relates to the ideas presented by the composer '. This does not mean, of course, that his intention is to minimize the importance of invention in treatment as well as in the production of themes ; but the point had better be made as clear as possible : for therein lies the difference between eloquence and mere rhetoric.

An instructive instance of the difficulties attending any attempt to demonstrate the difference was provided, some years ago, by a French critic who declared, in many pages of arguments and quotations, that a Sonata by a certain French composer of repute consisted entirely of borrowed materials and commonplace devices. His contribution, despite its unquestionable tightness, did not make very convincing reading even for people who agreed with him that the Sonata was unoriginal. To seek evidence in a text, first *totidem sententiis* and then *totidem verbis, syllabis,* or even *totidem litteris,* is a practice whose evils have been exposed long ago. But often enough, the choice for the musical critic lies between this and pure affirmation.

5

In order to determine the possible value of evidence of unoriginality, we might start by dividing the question, and deal separately with plagiarism, conscious or unconscious (quite apart from any question of ethics which might arise), of materials used or of methods of using them, and seek the boundary between the imitations and borrowings that matter and those that do not. We might say that in principle, to use sequences of sevenths is no more imitating any composer who happens to have first used them than resorting to combinations of consonant triads and dissonances is imitating anybody—unless indeed we posit that the latter is the high-road in harmony, and the former a by-way, a no-thoroughfare into which one composer has strayed; that to construct an operatic score on leitmotives is no more an act of imitation than to adopt the traditional scheme for a symphony, and so on. But this can be carried on *usque ad infinitum* and entails a postulate at almost each step; it will never tell us where the difference lies between a genuine work of art and a counterfeit.

In *What is Art ?* Clive Bell writes : ' A literal copy ' (of a painting) leaves us cold. . . . Yet if it were an ' absolutely exact copy, clearly it would be as moving ' as the original. . . . The explanation seems to be that ' the actual lines and colours and spaces in a work of

' art are caused by something in the mind of the artist
' which is not present in the mind of the imitator '
(p. 59). This is the only possible reply. All we can
do is to say, in Hadow's words, that a poor composer
' gives us design but not poetry ', or that his music
strikes us as uninspired. The last word remains with
the imagination. This naturally applies to the detec-
tion of all kinds of mechanical processes.

Supposing a composer has felt the need to treat
a theme polyphonically. All the methods of doing
so—imitations regular and irregular, direct and inverted, partial and total, by augmentation and by
diminution—are, in principle, equally satisfactory from
the purely rational point of view. Yet the composer
will resort to certain of these, and reject certain others.
Inverted, his theme will lose none of the features
(tonal and structural balance, similarity or contrast
with other elements used in the work, &c.) by virtue
of which it proved, in its original form, satisfactory
to the intellect. But he may feel that to use it in
that form would fulfil no artistic purpose, would be
out of keeping. Where the intellect can determine
no reasons for preference between possible forms, he
is able to decide by his sense of artistic fitness. The
origin of his preference lies in something in his mind
which would not have been present if he had proceeded
mechanically.

And nothing but a sense of artistic fitness will enable
the critic to keep pace with him. The problem of
distinguishing between an imitation and an original is
thus seen not to differ from the problem of telling
genuine art from bad art.

6

It may be alleged that the amount of skill displayed
in execution deserves consideration. The student
should satisfy himself whether the display of skill can
ever be considered as an end, not merely as a means.

108

Saint-Saëns was fond of saying that 'whoever cannot 'enjoy a sequence of chords merely because it is 'beautifully written does not deserve to be named 'a musician'. In the difference of outlook on this point lies one of the reasons why some people see vitality in music that to others is a mere collection of commonplaces. It is admitted by the latter that skill provides but the thinnest disguise for lack of genuine substance.

Lack of skill may certainly stand in the way of an artist's expressing himself adequately. It is far more important for the critic to know when this happens (apart from the question how the knowledge may affect his verdict) than to be influenced by skill displayed. Let it be remembered, however, that in music as in criticism, skill may turn a bad case into a very close imitation of a good one.

7

Forming judgements—as distinct from wording judgements—is essentially a question of acumen combined with consistency and flexibility. It is the outcome of 'the kind of intellectual sympathy by which 'we place ourselves within an object in order to 'coincide with what is unique in it, and therefore 'inexpressible', as Bergson has put it. This in turn depends upon the capacity to see the various aspects of every problem : first, no doubt, by considering its terms, but to no slight extent by considering the solutions which other critics offer or tend to—perhaps unconsciously. In other words, it is useful for the critic and not only for the tiro, to read a good deal of criticism on the very matters he has to deal with. Some critics object to this practice. They fear that to read other people's views may influence them, disturb them, lead them to plagiarize, and so forth. There are also those who feel sure that they have nothing to learn from others.

Critics endowed with the definiteness of purpose and discipline of mind needful to their calling need entertain no fear of being disturbed and influenced except where precisely it may be of service to them. If they feel in duty bound to adopt some other person's way of putting things, they will never experience any difficulty in knowing when the time comes for a quotation with due acknowledgement.

8

How long should a critic study a work before judging it—that is, when his duties as a critic are not interfered with by his duties as a journalist? The reply is : until he has satisfied himself that he has duly considered all points which may bear upon his judgement.) He is to feel confident in his power, in his choice of standards, in the consistency of his practice. If then he is reasonably sure that nothing in the work considered seems to render special caution desirable, he may pronounce even after one hearing or reading, knowing his judgement to be, so far as he is concerned, final, and decide then and there never to give the matter another thought. The responsibility lies with him; and he must be prepared to face the consequences.

It is sometimes argued that writers who hold works by X cheap (here X may stand for Brahms or Stravinsky or Bartòk or Tchaikovsky—it does not matter in the least) do not know his music well enough, and should have studied it with greater care. Arguments such as : ' you have not given X's music enough thought ', or, ' you are incapable of understanding X's music ', are unanswerable. They may be justified by facts. But unless substantiated by an adequate demonstration (not always easy to bring forth) they are inadmissible in criticism. Again, a time always comes when a critic is satisfied that he has pronounced his judgement and considered all possible grounds of appeal, and accordingly dismisses the matter from his mind. The more sensitive his imagination, and the greater his experience, the sooner he will reach this stage. Then, having passed judgement against a work, he will possibly forget all about this work until he sees fresh cause to reconsider it—which cause will not necessarily be the fact that others praise the work. Having pronounced, and knowing that as a music-lover he has no more use for the work than he has as a critic, he will perhaps find it better to keep all his attention for matters that prove to him less barren. Eventually, he may be unable to quote or recognize one bar of the work, or even to name the key in which the work is written. This will provide no valid argument against his pronouncement. He may find, however, that arguments will try his equanimity—which perhaps will be precisely the object of those who use them against him.

There are critics whose readiness to resort to the ' you-don't-understand ' form of challenging is equalled only by their indignation when the same weapon is used against themselves. It is only when there is truth in the allegation that the time comes to ascribe any importance to it : for then it constitutes a needful, if unpalatable, warning.

But if the critic knows how to judge and when to judge to the best of his ability and beliefs, he need not be perturbed, and all he can do is to stick to his guns. If any judgement of his happens to be of the kind of which examples are quoted on pp. 81–3 above, perhaps it will be his misfortune rather than his fault.

CHAPTER III

WORDING JUDGEMENTS

A. *The Principles*

I

THE story is told of a youthful composer who, having asked Mozart how to write a symphony, received the reply that he was too young to attempt anything of the kind. ' But, Master,' he said, ' had ' you not written many symphonies long before you ' reached my present age?' ' Yes,' Mozart retorted ; ' but then I did not ask how it was to be done.'

It is extremely unlikely that the novice who takes up musical criticism instinctively—not merely as an alternative to any other profession or branch of writing —will be tempted to ask how to write his criticisms. Indeed, he may eagerly seek advice on the matter of forming his judgements and yet fail to realize the difficulties, technical, ethical, and tactical, of the art of wording judgements. This wording must illustrate the spirit in which every judgement is arrived at ; and this spirit, when all is said and done, is the only thing that really matters. It is no paradox to say that in a judgement—and especially in the individual judgement which it is the critic's business to provide—the sentence passed may be the writer's ultimate object and the readers' ultimate expectation, but the actual importance and interest lie in the elucidations, arguments, and suggestions that gave rise to it and substantiate it ; all the difference between genuine criticism and mere talk consists therein.

Here the needful experience will prove far easier to acquire than experience in forming judgements ; for it is chiefly a matter of common sense, tact, and sense of proportion.

First and foremost, a good deal depends upon the critic's proposed object. This object, in theory, is simple enough : it is to see how far and why he considers a work good or bad, and to pronounce accordingly ; to define as plainly as possible the position, merits, and demerits of composers and others, to show the issue of tendencies and to offer solutions of various art problems, or contribute to their solution.

In practice, things are far less simple. Very fortunately, the critic is not actually invested with the functions of judge or jury, and the last say does not rest with him. He may make a show of passing sentence ; but in point of fact he is only telling others how, in his mind, sentence should be passed. His dicta carry weight only so far as he can prove every point, or persuade by sheer force or subtlety of eloquence. Therefore, even if he restricts his aims to passing judgement, he must bear his real position in mind and proceed accordingly, playing his part as counsel and witness whenever need arises. Upon him devolves the care of discovering, adducing, and interpreting the evidence upon which the judgement rests.

A critic who takes a broad and thorough view of his duties may even hold himself bound to champion certain views or certain works, to attack certain others. He may wish to play a part as an educator, possibly as a propagandist of that which he loves. He may consider it desirable not to wait for cases to be brought to his notice, but deliberately to seek them in the past as well as in the present.

In these various instances, he may restrict his ambitions to making his point to his own satisfaction, or, on the contrary, wish to convince others. The mere

H

scoring of bull's-eyes, towards which cleverness in dialectics and in the art of writing may prove more useful even than sound judgement and sympathetic discrimination, is one thing, and the kind of work which stimulates and assists the reader another. It is quite possible, of course, to be carried too far by the desire to carry conviction ; but the critic who fights shy of considering how his judgements are best substantiated and made acceptable does so at his own peril and at that of the cause he has undertaken to vindicate.

3

In order to decide how to dispose his batteries, the critic should begin by knowing which public he is addressing and which order of influence he wishes to exercise. He may be writing for readers with no specialized knowledge and slight experience, if any, or for the experienced fraction of the public, or for actual students or brother specialists. Hence the temptation to say that his writings will fall under one of the three headings : (*a*) of interest to the layman but not to the specialist ; (*b*) of interest to the specialist but not to the layman ; (*c*) of interest to both. For a critic, however, there is no swifter road to perdition than to believe there is an excuse for writing stuff which perforce will have to go in category (*a*) or (*b*). If his ideas are of any value, even his primers or short notices, however elementary, will be good enough to interest the expert reader. And if he is capable of clear thinking and clear writing, his learned essays and fat tomes will be read with interest and profit by any non-specialist sufficiently educated to understand his utterances and mode of thought.

Whether you write for educated music-lovers or for music-lovers in the elementary stages of education, all essentials remain unchanged. The wording is of importance simply because your object is to be under-

114

stood. To make the point clear, let us suppose that your article contains musical illustrations : if you have reason to suppose that your public can read scores, you need not resort to examples transcribed in pianoforte form—which you would naturally do in the opposite case. Exactly thus should you adapt the form of your arguments to the requirements of those whom you address.

Nothing illustrates the importance of adapting one's writings to one's readers better than the correspondence or articles from abroad which appear in many musical periodicals. These are—with exceptions of course—among the feeblest and to the average reader least interesting contributions in the paper. The reason lies in the differences in points of view : between the publics of two respective countries (the most educated fractions as well as the least) there are countless differences of outlook, education, sensitiveness, and habits of thought. Writers from abroad, who are at a disadvantage through not knowing the atmosphere in which their articles will be read, may carry their point in thorough-going essays, but will fail to do so under the conditions of summary brevity which are the rule in contributions of that kind. What they ask their readers to take for granted differs from what their readers are prepared to take for granted. The measure of common opinion is not what either side thinks it is. This often occurs even when expert critics of one country read the work of critics of another. Despite the current opinion that music is the most universal of arts, the fact is that in the appraisement of music national idiosyncrasies, as a rule, play a far greater part than in the appraisement of other arts. This is shown, for instance, by comparing what is generally thought and written of Liszt, Brahms, Fauré, Scriabin, and Tchaikovsky in Russia, Britain, and France respectively. But even when writing for people whose outlook is in the main similar to your own, it is well to remember that your work will be fruitful only so far as it invites the reader's co-operation by appealing to him and interesting him.

4

✓The critic's plan of action may be primarily to persuade or to convince, to educate or to kindle enthusiasm ; it may be to dictate or to suggest opinions or to enable the readers to form opinions of their own. His ambition may be restricted to dealing efficiently with the topic of the moment, or it may be to contribute, so far as possible, towards laying a foundation for something bigger and more enduring, for a ' fresh force in criticism '.

But above all he should ask himself whether he is going to tell the readers what to think of music which they know or may find access to, or calling their attention to music which they do not know and have no means of knowing. A moment's reflection will tell him that this order of consideration, which of course has not the slightest bearing upon his judgements, is very important with regard to the form in which he should elect to express them.

Clive Bell, in *Since Cézanne* (pp. 154 sq.), says that ' primarily, the critic is a sign-post. He points to ' a work of art and says : " Stop, look ! " . . . Con- ' fronting a work which stimulates his enthusiasm, he ' can do little more than jump for joy.' If we admit that aesthetic judgement rests on the imagination far more than on the intellect, we must agree with him, and say conversely, that when confronting a work which he does not like, the critic can do little more than shudder with disgust. According as we think that analysis may be helpful, we may qualify these two statements ; but let us for the time being accept them as they stand.

If you write about works which your readers do not know, your course is fairly clear. But one point of ethics arises which may be disposed of at once. When you write in praise of a work, the worst that may happen is that after becoming acquainted with that work your readers may disagree with you, and your reputation as a critic will suffer accordingly. You alone will bear the brunt of your mistake—if mistake it be. Therefore, when you are prepared to take the risk, you need have no scruple about expressing yourself as forcibly as you wish to. But if you are consigning to perdition a work to which your public may not easily have access, it is necessary to exercise greater caution. In proportion as your influence is greater, your verdict may help in preventing performance or study of the works you condemn ; and it is only by being performed and studied broadcast that works get fair play.

An instance of apparent unfairness occurs in a certain primer on musical appreciation with reference to Liszt. The facts of the case are that the author offers objections to Liszt's methods in terms copied word for word from an article by Parry in Grove's *Dictionary*, without making it clear that he is quoting from it. To all intents and purposes, the opinion thus expressed seems to be the outcome of his own thinking, until, encountering the same ideas, identically worded, in the *Dictionary*, we are led to wonder how far the author of the primer has actually threshed out matters himself. He may have (and let us hope he has) done so ; but had he inserted in the condemnatory paragraph the words ' as Parry points out ', he would not even incur the suspicion of having failed in his duties. As it happens, Liszt's main works are included neither in the current repertory of concerts nor in the usual curriculum of students ; so that censures of that kind, disseminated in books intended for elementary instruction, may exercise a far greater influence than what might be written on works with which the British public is more familiar.

When 'jumping for joy' in honour of a known work, or holding it up to execration, you may be writing in accordance with the prevailing view or against it. Now suppose that you are urging your readers to amend the unfavourable opinion they entertain of works which you think highly of : you are promising them something positive, an addition to the range of their enjoyment. They may wonder at finding works which leave them cold described as thrilling and lovable, yet eventually be swayed by the inducement held out.

On the contrary, if you are trying to make people see that their taste and faith is at fault, the position is that you are holding out no direct, positive inducement : ostensibly, you are proposing, not to add to their stock of artistic pleasure, but to detract from it. The task is as graceless as that of taking a bone from a dog. In all likelihood, you will find that you are preaching in the desert, and that your readers incline to dispose of the matter by telling themselves that they know better, and perhaps to apply to your exertions the stupid and meaningless epithet ' high-brow '. If you are to convince them at all, it will be by dint of the utmost caution and wisdom. The point is to make them realize that a weakness for inferior types, more or less harmful in all arts, is absolutely fatal in music, because the evolution of our musical taste depends entirely upon our musical experiences : nothing outside music will provide correctives such as are provided in the matter of literature by the general education of our minds, or in that of the fine arts by the experiences of our senses in contact with the outer world. Wordsworth is reported to have alleged that ' a stupid invention, in prose or verse, is quite harmless '. Knowing how much smaller the average man's capacity for and chances of assimilating music are than with literature and the other arts, how very much less varied his musical experiences are than any others, one could hardly say the same with reference to the stupid inventions in music with which the world is overrun. Judicious criticism, therefore, has a great and much-needed part to play with regard to the extirpation of bad music.

There are two ways only towards this end. The critic may ruthlessly dissect the alleged bad music, with the hope of awakening in his readers something of his own sense of reality and proportion, or he may resort to comparisons between bad and good, if he is able to hit upon one that is telling enough. In his chapter on Criticism, Clive Bell (*Since Cézanne*, p. 173) points out that ' discriminating critics alone extract light from refuse, and deal profitably with bad art '. He continues by telling how a critic, by analysing ' with magisterial severity ' the works of a poet for whom a lady professed an admiration which this critic thought unjustified, and by recommending a comparison with the works of another and in his opinion better poet, succeeded in altering that lady's views. Likewise does W. J. Turner (*Music and Life*, p. 112) end his denunciation of Charpentier's *Louise* with the words :

' If you find you like it, put on sackcloth and ashes
' and listen to Beethoven and Brahms and Debussy and
' Rimsky-Korsakof and Wagner . . . until you feel
' what is wrong with *Louise* . . . for then and then
' only will you be a man who *hears*, and not a mere
' receptacle of stray sounds.'

The way in which a critic deals with music which he considers bad should be the acid test of his professional capacity. It often occurs that a critic contributes more useful matter when speaking of works which he likes than when speaking of works which he dislikes. There are good reasons why it should be thus ; for no human being is without his blind spot, and concentration upon a topic may lead to a development of the blind spot as well as of the range and acuity of vision. It has already been explained that when a critic is satisfied that he has no use for certain works, he may be justified in ceasing to devote attention to them. But meanwhile others, who think otherwise, will perhaps achieve, by continued study, valuable results of which he will have renounced all possibility. If he elects to take his stand thus, he should not be surprised to find his views eventually superseded. Whether right or wrong in his hates and loves, the critic will find that whereas it is fairly easy to be convincing when 'jumping for joy', it is still easier to miss the mark when shuddering with disgust. Sweeping assertions and facile methods such as poking fun are tempting, and may be useful; but neither heavy artillery nor vicious little machine-guns will carry the day unless mounted on the broadest and firmest of foundations and fired with unerring accuracy and economy. Analyses and comparisons will tell only if their wording is as accurate as their principle is sound. In short, the task of dealing with music which one does not like will often call for an infinitely greater amount of time, labour, and caution than any other within the musical critic's province. It is often accomplished somewhat perfunctorily. Incidentally, it may be pointed out that the importance, from the educational point of view, of a close study of 'bad' music is overlooked by all writers on musical appreciation. One reason probably is that these writers feel that the question why music is bad cannot be disposed of in a few vague generalities such as are held to serve the purpose of explaining why music is good.

6

That critical utterances should be specific, and not consist of stereotyped generalities which at their best might refer to a thousand works as well as to the

120

particular work under notice, and at their worst to
a novel or a picture or a drama as well as to music,
is of course always desirable. Practically all that could
be said on this point is summed up in the following
lines from Clive Bell's *Since Cézanne* (p. 97) :

' Any student proposing to educate himself as a critic
' should be compelled to devote the first years of his
' course to the criticism of non-representative art . . .
' he will find himself obliged to explore the depths of
' his own aesthetic experience. To explain honestly
' why he prefers this chair to that requires, he will
' find, a far more intense effort of the intellect and
' imagination than any amount of fine writing about
' portraits and landscapes. . . . He will be driven into
' that world of minute differences and subtle reactions
' which is the world of art.'

For the word chair substitute the word ' sonata ',
and for ' portraits and landscapes ' the words ' fate-
knocking-at-the-door ', and you have it all in a nutshell. Technical analysis, however, has its stereotypes
as well as emotional paraphrase. These are all the
more dangerous because they appear specific to the
unwary or untrained eye. The student should think
over these principles formulated by Gayley and
Scott :

' Many definitions of poetry mistake the poetic
' faculty for the art ; some definitions limiting them-
' selves to its nature, and others to its aims, fail to
' distinguish poetry from art in general ; no definition
' is adequate which does not characterize (1) the sub-
' ject of treatment, (2) the form of expression, and
' (3) the process of execution.'

The comments and scheme of investigation which
follow (pp. 280 sq.) will be found extremely useful.

It is equally needful to be specific in the wording
of whatever description is given of the music referred

to and in the wording of judgements. Whenever the need is felt to refer to some definite standard—for example, when speaking of form, of scoring, and so forth—ambiguity should be carefully avoided, for the reason given in the chapters on standards and data. Nothing could be more deceptive than the colour of finality which judgements assume when they appear to refer to facts.

CHAPTER IV

WORDING JUDGEMENTS (*continued*)

B. *The Application*

I

THE outcome of the foregoing remarks is that your wording should be forcible, specific, and so far as needful circumstantial, so as to ensure unambiguity, consistency, and, above all things, adjustment of the means to the end. Even if we decide that criticism is an art, as Blaikie Murdoch and others allege (see *supra*, p. 29), we must acknowledge that its methods differ from those of purely creative art so far as the critic must keep in view the possible effect of his writings on others. For the creative artist, to know that he is right from his own point of view is enough. The critic, unless led by egotism or aloofness to take a merely academic interest in the making of his point, will wish to take what steps he can to make it acceptable even to those who are indifferent or hostile. The very desire to hold out inducements—so far as this can be done without swerving from one's beliefs— which has spelt ruin for many a gifted creative artist, may help the critic to achieve his ends for the greater good of both his reputation and of the causes which he espouses.

Clive Bell rightly says that ' Canons in criticism are
' as unessential as subjects in painting. . . . The critic's
' end (to which a variety of means are equally good)
' is to bring his spectator before a work of art in an
' alert and sympathetic frame of mind. . . . It matters
' hardly at all what words the critic employs provided
' they have the power of infecting his audience with

123

' his genuine enthusiasm ' (*Since Cézanne*, pp. 156–8).
But it is not always easy to know how this purpose is
best fulfilled.

If a book on criticism could be written in the same
spirit as a Treatise on Rhetoric, this would be the
place for a description, in tabular form, of the various
kinds of criticism, narrative, analytical, technically
descriptive, poetically descriptive, and so forth, with
due reference to their respective merits and demerits.
But it is neither needful nor desirable to instruct
would-be critics in the art of word-spinning—which
they generally acquire long before they acquire any
other. Whichever suggestions on these various methods
appeared useful have been offered or implied in the
theoretical part of this book.

One paramount order of consideration, however,
remains to be touched : the space at the writer's
disposal, and the various other special conditions
created by the form which the publication of his
work will take.

Obviously, the remarks offered in this chapter and
the foregoing apply to the body and general trend of
the critic's work more than to any particular piece of
work. Needless to say that they are not intended for
the writer of short notices at short notice—a graceless
task, but all in the day's work for most professional
critics, many of whom strive to do good work, and
often much-needed spade-work, under adverse circumstances. This class of work is all the more worthy of
interest for the fact that it reaches the greatest fraction
of that general public with whom the critic desirous
of furthering the cause of art should be concerned first
and last. To write for brother specialists, as I have
said already, is a laudable practice—criticism indeed
may be described as one of the very few provinces in
which it proves profitable to take in one another's
washing. But the main issue is always to stimulate
and to instruct the public at large.

124

'Nonsense'; 'A masterpiece'; 'Middling'; 'Sound but unoriginal ' : these apparently most unambiguous judgements are the acme of ambiguity except in one respect which may or may not be of interest to the reader. As they stand, they merely mean that a writer (identified or not) entertains a certain view of a certain work. They may be the outcome of countless years of experience and weeks of anxious thought, or may have been dashed off by the veriest ignoramus. The result is all one : if you do not know who wrote, the value of the judgement, to you, is exactly *nil*. Supposing your critical pabulum to consist solely of such tabloids, miscellaneous in origin, the result will be, where judgements differ, a feeling of helplessness and bewilderment ; where they agree, the impression that no other opinion can exist.

If the judgements you habitually read emanate from one critic, and you know that they do, you may begin to see light. By comparing his views on works which you know with your own, you will acquire some kind of insight into his standards and taste, and accordingly ascribe some more or less definite meaning to his utterances on works which you do not know. This, at best, is a precarious standard. For instance, practically every one agrees on the great majority of works belonging to the past—the boundary of common agreement, so to speak, may be fixed somewhere in the neighbourhood of 1850, with a few marked deflexions here and there. It is impossible to speak of anything like universal agreement as to the works of Liszt, Brahms, Mussorgsky, Mahler, and many others ; and controversy is rife with regard to Scriabin, Ravel, Bartòk, Stravinsky, and Schönberg. In short, the utmost we may know of a writer's consistency will hardly enable the shrewdest of us to foretell the effect upon him of music of an unwonted kind.

Enough has been said to show the disadvantages

under which the writer of short notices labours. The sole value of his utterances resides in the individuality behind them. If he publishes in the same paper short notices and, occasionally, long articles in which he deals as thoroughly as possible with points of importance, it will be of great benefit to the reader as well as to himself, and lead to better understanding. But in any case it is a great pity that the practice of anonymous criticism should still obtain in many papers, here and elsewhere. It has the further disadvantage of rendering it practically compulsory to utter judgements in dogmatic, axiomatic form, and of precluding the occasional use of the first person or of other modes of implying a restriction which at times might make all the difference, not only between fairness and unfairness, but between what has meaning and what has not.

The only criticism which will lose nothing by anonymity is that which is circumstantial and thorough enough to leave no point in the dark. For instance, the essay in the *Edinburgh Review* from which several quotations have been given here would be equally illuminating had its authorship not ceased to be a secret. And the test of a good book—be it a primer or a full treatise—is that we never need devote a thought to the question, by whom was it written? In other words, it is the author's idiosyncrasies that account for all that is left to be taken for granted : ideal criticism, which leaves nothing to be taken for granted, is rarely to be found. Nor, of course, is this ideal criticism needful under all circumstances. But it is imperative for the critic to be understood and trusted.

3

The chief difficulty with which the critic has to contend is the inadequacy and looseness of the vocabulary at his disposal, for the purposes of describing as well as of judging.

It is generally impossible to describe music in words. At times a specific technical description is possible (especially of single points), but comparatively seldom. And even when it is, its critical import will remain limited. The effects produced by music may be described impressively, but not always with sufficient accuracy to constitute a contribution to criticism.

The following instance of technical analysis, cleverly effected and fulfilling its purpose excellently, refers to the transition from the Scherzo to the Finale in Beethoven's Fifth Symphony :

‘ The motive of the Scherzo reappears, pizzicato. ‘ We gradually revert to silence, except for a few notes ‘ lightly plucked on the violins and the strange little ‘ cackles of the bassoons giving the high A flat which ‘ sharply clashes with the G, octave of the ground- ‘ note of the chord of minor dominant ninth. Then, ‘ breaking with the rhythm, the strings (this time with ‘ the bow) gently strike the chord of A flat and rest ‘ on it. Alone the kettledrums keep up the rhythm, ‘ the sponge-damped drumsticks striking gentle thuds ‘ which hardly break the repose of all the other instru- ‘ ments. The note they give is C. The piece is in ‘ C minor, but the harmony of A flat, long kept up ‘ by the other instruments, seems to introduce a new ‘ key while the faint but distinct tattoo of the kettle- ‘ drums tends to maintain the feeling of the original ‘ key. The ear is in doubt . . . you do not know where ‘ this harmonic mystery will lead to . . . but the ‘ muffled thuds grow louder by degrees ; the violins ‘ now take part in the motion and the harmony changes ‘ to that of the dominant seventh G B D F, while the ‘ kettledrums obstinately repeat the tonic C ; and the ‘ whole orchestra, including the trombones which had ‘ not yet appeared, raises in the major mode the theme ‘ of a triumphal march.’

(Berlioz, *A Travers Chants*, p. 33.)

Notice how exactly the above lines describe what takes place and how truly they convey the effect produced. The description is a model of soberness. It does not contain a single epithet, allusion, or simile introduced for the deliberate purpose of suggesting ideas or emotions. Strip it of its technicalities or suppose it to be read by some one who does not know what such terms as C, G, pizzicato, ground-note, or dominant ninth mean, and its significance will remain.

There are cases when no hope of achieving anything of the kind can be entertained. At times the complexity of the music will baffle endeavour. At others, it will be its very simplicity. Take the little motive which appears in the third act of *Siegfried* and plays a leading part in *Siegfried Idyll* :

try to think out a way of expressing its subtle pregnancy and surpassing loveliness ; try, by alluding to melody or harmony or rhythm or colour, to explain its utter originality. The only thing you can do, you will soon find, is to ' jump for joy '.

4

In his *Essays on English Literature*, Professor Saintsbury says (ch. ix) that the test of a criticism's value is the question, what idea of the original would this criticism give to a tolerably instructed person who does not know the original? As regards music, we may say with confidence that usually no person, even more than tolerably instructed, will come near acquiring a fair idea of the original unless that person is acquainted with the critic's outlook. And we know that it is not always possible for the critic to help in this respect. Most terms in which judgements may be expressed are as unsatisfactory as those which serve only to describe. The only way to dispose so far as possible of their looseness and vagueness lies in a careful and ruthless analysis of every term in the critic's vocabulary.

This analysis will generally reveal how far a judgement is founded on facts and how far a matter of mere opinion.

Take the judgement on the scherzo of a symphony quoted on pp. 103–4: to the remark that unless the facts are true the judgement is most unfair may be added that the facts themselves are not altogether final. Knocking a beat out of a metrical pattern may be a stroke of inspiration, not a mechanical makeshift. The import of the criticism lies in the word 'halting' and in the implication that the outcome is laboured. Analysis reveals that in principle both constitute judgements rather than statements of actual facts. As regards the term 'halting', however, the distinction is theoretical rather than real: for a critic for whom the difference between halting rhythm (unintentionally halting, of course) and flowing rhythm is not a reality had better seek another outlet for his energies than criticism. But not so as regards the term 'laboured'.

Referring to Fétis's assertion that in the *Tannhäuser* Overture 'beyond a poor, ill-harmonized chorale-tune 'there is not a spark of melody in the whole produc-'tion', Hadow (*Essays in Modern Music*) writes : 'To 'have passed over Tannhäuser's song is fatal. There 'it stands in the middle of the allegro, a complete

' 32-bar tune, in as clear, perfect, and unmistakable
' a stanza as " La ci darem " or " God save the
' Queen ". There may be differences of opinion as to
' its merits . . . but to deny its existence is simply
' to put oneself out of court on a matter of fact.'

We may say that when speaking of melody Fétis,
if he meant anything at all, gave the word a meaning
very different from that which Hadow gives it in
this crushing confutation : he probably used it as
a synonym for certain particular lilts and commonplaces without which, in his mind, no ' tune ' could
exist.

To describe a tune as ill-harmonized may mean
that the harmonies do not follow one another in
accordance with school rules, or that the part-writing
is clumsy, or that the harmonies fail to satisfy the
ear, or that they clash with the character of the tune
as conceived by the critic, and a great many other
things. In music written otherwise than in accordance
with the usual principles of tonality and part-writing,
it is bound to be a mere matter of opinion. Even
with reference to ordinary tonal music, it is not always
conclusive—as shown, for example, by the same Fétis's
dismay upon finding an ' irregular ' chord used by
Mozart (see *supra*, p. 82).

Even where it seems that judgement should be
entirely a matter of facts we find that experts differ
in the principles or the spirit according to which they
pronounce. Hadow (*Essays in Modern Music*) writes
that ' Berlioz ranks with Beethoven, Wagner, and
' Dvořák, as one of the four greatest masters of Instru-
' mentation that the world has ever seen '. We feel
that his point of view is different from that of the
critic who, called upon to name these four, would
unhesitatingly include Liszt, Rimsky-Korsakof, or
Saint-Saëns rather than Beethoven and Dvořák. As
regards the former especially, we see Rimsky-Korsakof
in the Preface to his *Treatise of Orchestration* adducing

facts with which it seems hard to reconcile Hadow's view. ' Beethoven's gigantic personality ', he writes, ' is a thing apart. His music embodies the power- ' ful sway of a profound and inexhaustible orchestral ' imagination ; but the execution, so far as details are ' concerned, lags far behind the titanic conceptions. ' The trumpet parts stand out, the horns are given ' difficult and unfavourable intervals ; the writing for ' strings is splendid, the way in which the woodwinds ' are used often makes for fine colours ; but the whole ' is such as to afford the student many occasions ' for bewilderment.' Long before Rimsky-Korsakof's treatise had appeared, a shrewd though irreverent French critic, Émile Vuillermoz, had remarked that the trumpet part of a Beethoven symphony ' consisted ' essentially of three hundred repetitions or so of the ' tonic, and about two hundred of the dominant '.

Comparing Hadow's view with Rimsky-Korsakof's, we realize that the word ' scoring ', upon which both judgements hinge, admits of more constructions than one. Is the test of good scoring to be found merely in the general impression of power, fitness, and colour conveyed by the music, or in the adaptation of the means to the end—in such facts as, for instance, that the music can be played exactly as written, without any undue effort being called for, and will sound exactly as the writing shows that the composer intended it to sound? It is obvious that for Rimsky-Korsakof the scope of the term is essentially technical ; whereas Hadow is probably thinking of instrumentation not *per se*, but in conjunction with other things, such as, say, the substance, style, and tone of the music, and pronouncing upon them jointly. The two writers are not on common ground. Whether Rimsky-Korsakof, with his more accurate delineation of his meaning, stands on safer ground than Hadow is a question which no reader can usefully consider unless he possesses enough technical and other knowledge to weigh the *pros* and *cons* of either standpoint. But certainly the layman, even after having read both statements, will see no reason why he should accept the one rather than the other.

5

Nothing could be more hopelessly equivocal than what is written with regard to form in music. To deal efficiently with the topic would require far more space than it can be given here. But an instance or two will provide at least the necessary warning.

For some writers, the word form merely means conformity to certain standard types ; and if a work is neither in Overture form, nor in Sonata form, nor in Rondo form, nor any other duly classified form, those writers describe it as formless. Others hold that form depends upon a certain modulatory order, and cannot exist, for instance, in a work which does not end in the key in which it had begun. For others, the term stands for consistency, balance, and, above all things, continuity of interest. Thus Ernest Newman (*Sunday Times*, 30 December 1922) rightly says : ' The form of a musical work is good when the work ' is neither too short nor too long for its subject, and ' when each bar of the music follows logically on the ' bar before it and leads logically into the bar that ' comes after it.' The only word which this definition leaves unexplained is the word ' logically ', which every one can and will interpret according to his own lights.

Another excellent definition by the same writer (*Sunday Times*, 17 October 1921) is that good form consists of ' the perfect balance of the idea, the sub- ' stance, and the means. . . . We want to feel not only ' that there is not a superfluous note in the work . . . ' but that every fragment of it is working towards ' a divinely preappointed end.' Lascelles Aber- crombie's definition (*An Essay towards a Theory of*

132

Art) expresses the same truth in equally forcible terms :

' The significance which form carries is the significance
' it gives to the matter it forms . . . any artistic form
' is significant which expresses the unity of its matter.'

But would anybody venture to say that form, thus conceived, is a matter of bare fact to be judged as such, and not from the point of view of aesthetic imagination, apart from all tangible landmarks as described in text-books ?

The latent ambiguity of the word form gives rise to many vain discussions on form *versus* formalism. Scott Goddard, in the *Musical News and Herald* (May 1922), described Brahms as the last of the great formalists, explaining the assertion as follows : ' Brahms
' was so imbued with the idea that once a melody had
' appeared it had to be worked upon, inverted, com-
' bined with other melodies, that he seems, at times,
' to have used a tune for its desirability as a vehicle
' for contrapuntal devices rather than for its beauty
' of inspired form ; and, slave to his ancestry, to have
' pinched and cut, docked and deformed, his tunes
' in order to fit them into " a scheme ".' Scott Goddard's definition is unequivocal enough. Obviously formalism to him means a tendency to be governed by certain customs, as distinct from the actual resort to certain devices. He uses the term with reference, not to the fact that certain means are used, but to the spirit which leads to their being employed. And he certainly tells us that in his opinion there are in Brahms's works fragments which do not ' work towards a divinely preappointed end '.

Ernest Newman, challenging this view, wrote (in the *Sunday Times*) :

' What *is* formalism, in the last resort, but a way that
' men have found out of doing things with the mini-
' mum of waste and the maximum of effect ? . . . It

I 3

' is not only the friend of expression, but the indispens-
' able ally of it. . . . Expression implies a discipline as
' well as a wealth of feeling, which discipline in turn
' implies a formalism of some kind.'

Here we cannot help feeling that a valuable distinction is done away with. If we accept Newman's
definition, we shall have to find some other way of
expressing the fact that certain things in music seem
to be the outcome of routine rather than of actual
creative imagination. Newman contrasts formalism,
in the favourable sense which he gives to the word,
with formalism carried to excess. So far as mere
nomenclature is concerned, it does not matter in the
least whether we call a thing formalism, or excess of
formalism, or abracadabra, provided we are able to
establish a sharp distinction between the judicious use
of formal devices, so far as they serve the composer's
purpose independently conceived, and mere assuetude
to convention and routine. Without the former there
can be no great work of art. Its antithesis is the
incapacity to use the principles of form as means
towards an end, which may become manifest in two
ways : the composer either giving us something un-
shaped and inorganic, or copying a formal pattern
instead of evolving one or—which comes to the same—
making us accept as necessary the one which he adopts.

Since, when all is said and done, formalism, as
defined by Newman, must needs exist in all works
of art worthy of consideration, why not emphasize as
strongly as possible the difference between works which
exemplify mastery of form and works which are the
outcome of enslavement to form by reserving the term
formalism for the latter?

Here the analysis of terms provided by both writers
has helped to thresh matters out. But how are we
to account for the discrepancies between the following
statements ?—

134

(*a*) ' Brahms evinces a fairly characteristic tendency
' to renovate the Sonata form, . . . the cyclic principle
' is latent in his imperfect attempts : it was to be
' carried to perfection almost exclusively by César
' Franck and the French school.' (Vincent d'Indy,
Treatise of Composition, ii. 418.)

' Franck's symphony is an unfaltering ascent towards
' pure joy and vivifying light, for its construction is
' firm . . .' (The same writer, *César Franck*, p. 153.)

(*b*) ' In Brahms's symphonies and in Franck's sym-
' phony the shortcomings originate in the same defect :
' lack of proportion between the ideas and the working-
' out.   With Brahms, the inspiration is clear and
' simple both in joyous and in melancholy moods ;
' the working-out is skilful, grandiloquent, involved,
' and heavy.   With Franck, the melody is lofty and
' serene, the harmony daring and wonderfully rich,
' but the form is appallingly poor.   He repeats groups
' of bars, or even whole pages, merely transposing
' them, and resorts immoderately to threadbare de-
' vices' (Ravel in *S. I. M.*—the monthly journal of the
French section of the International Music Society—
March 1912).

Again, both writers certainly know the subject.
They use the same terms without giving us any reason
to suppose that they ascribe different meanings to
them, and yet there appears to be no common ground
between the two.   Be he a layman or an expert, the
reader is bound to come to the conclusion that judgements on form, in spite of appearances, are very much
more a matter of opinion than of facts.

6

Thus will the critic, patiently dissecting every term
which he wishes to use or finds others using, gradually
learn to conform, so far as is humanly possible, with
the ideal of perspicuity and appositeness described by

Robertson. As he proceeds, he will be surprised to find how difficult it is to calculate the exact range of his firing and the extent or strength of his defences. To find that he has wrought almost irreparable havoc where he was only intending to fire a warning shot, or that he is nearing collapse in proportion as he believes he is coming off with flying colours, may be unpleasant, but will teach him more, if he is conscientious, than any amount of mere theorizing. It is better for him to learn how to engineer his forces so as to take no risks blindly than to be made wise by others after the event. In the present state of knowledge, it is true, he runs no great risk of being found out ; nor will he run a greater until the time when the present state of arbitrariness and confusion no longer prevails.

He will also learn to husband his strength so as to strike more forcibly ; or rather, to bring this strength to bear upon the point where its effect will be truest and most thorough. Generally, it is when he gets excited and deals haphazard blows right and left that he accomplishes the least. A good deal can be done by the quietest methods. For instance, it is often possible, even when describing facts without obvious show of praise or disparagement, to point to the advantages or to the drawbacks which one sees. Compare, for instance, these two ways of characterizing Sonata-form, one of which lays stress upon its possibilities, the other upon its limitations :

' This is the highest type of structural development
' to which music has yet arrived. The three clauses
' of the primitive ballad-tune have grown into three
' cantos, all different in character and function, all
' working together in the maintenance of a single
' economy. The first, technically known as the Exposi-
' tion, presents two subjects or paragraphs, diverse in
' key, and connected by a short episodal link of modula-
' tion ; the second, technically known as the Develop-
' ment Section, consists of a fantasia on themes or

'phrases of the first, with such freedom of key as the
'composer choses to adopt; the third, technically
'known as the Recapitulation, repeats the two subjects
'with any minimum of change that may be implied
'in the transposition of the second to the tonic key.
'. . . It is hardly necessary to point out that the
'principle of perfect symmetry embodied in this form
'is precisely the same as that in which is constructed
'a great drama or a great novel. At the outset our
'attention is divided between two main centres of
'interest; as the work proceeds, the plan is com-
'plicated by the introduction of new centres; at its
'close, the complications are cleared away and the
'interests identified.' (Hadow, *Studies in Modern
Music*, ii, pp. 52–3.)

'A symphony is a contest, not between melodic or
'harmonic elements, but between keys. The opening
'movement begins by two motives entering the field.
'Each is the champion of a key. This is called the
'Exposition. The Development is a duel during
'which the antagonists in turn gain or lose ground.
'The issue is known beforehand: it is the second
'motive that will don the key introduced by its rival,
'and in this conciliating garb reappear in the third
'part or Recapitulation. The whole interest lies in
'the episodes, the lunging, feinting, thrusting, and
'parrying. The listener sits as umpire. And nothing
'diverts his sapient attention, for he knows from the
'very outset that it is E flat, or D major, to win.'
(L. Laloy, *Claude Debussy*, Paris, 1909, p. 65.)

It is also possible to state facts without interpreting
them, even when one's object is to make a point. In
the following example, the writer's intention is to
show the principle whose application illustrates the
logical order of the music he refers to. He does not
imply that the 'polarization' he describes is the cause
and mainspring of this order, nor that it is the best

possible or not ; he simply adduces it as the sign that happens to be available in the instance under notice. There is no trace of special pleading such as crops up in the quotation from Laloy above.

' The work's polyphony is not based upon tonality, ' but each section is, so to speak, polarized round ' a note or an interval which serves as a kind of nexus, ' and which is modulated in passing to the following ' section. It is intended thereby to secure harmonic ' unity without proceeding by a segment of the circle ' of keys ' (Edwin Evans, programme-notice on Stravinsky's *Symphonies d'Instruments à Vent*, 1921).

7

Although as a general rule the simplest wording is the best, the critic will occasionally find it necessary not to sacrifice accuracy to simplicity and brevity. His task is so very delicate that all may depend upon the selection of the right shade of meaning—which in turn may call for the use of an unusual or apparently clumsy expression instead of a simpler. Now and then the outcome will be as unpleasant to the reader as the application of a dentist's drill (there is, I fear, more than a little of the dentist's drill in this book), but the critic's art should be to make the readers see that the result will be no less beneficial. But as a rule the elaborate apparel of precautions recommended here is for his own protection. How much evidence of any of the steps that have led to his judgements should be allowed to appear in any of his writings is entirely a matter of time and circumstance ; and of this he will be the best judge. Anyhow, he must satisfy himself and his critics that he has acquired the right to express himself as briefly as he pleases, and the capacity to know when he may do so without obscurity or harm. When this is done, the readers will have to do their own share of the work. They must have learnt to understand criticism exactly as the critic has learnt to write it. He cannot be expected to perform their task as well as his own. If they lack the necessary minimum of discrimination, they will now and then go astray. But this will not be the critic's fault.

8

A question often asked is, how far should criticism resort to technical considerations or illustrations? The answer has already been given, at least partly. On the special point of wording, a few remarks may be added here by way of caution. The various quotations to be found in this book may be taken as fairly representative of the degree of technicality in which a writer may indulge without danger when addressing non-specialists. But this, again, is largely a matter of circumstance. The essential point is that no technical statement should be allowed to stand in lieu of argument. Some critics seem to think it possible to describe a tune as beautiful by saying that it is in the Mixolydian mode, or a modulation as unsatisfactory by pointing out its 'irregularity'. As was shown with reference to the quotation from Berlioz on p. 127, the test of a good piece of technical criticism is that it will stand unimpaired after the technicalities have been removed. Likewise, musical examples should be used as a rule solely to illustrate points made, and not in order to avoid the trouble or risk of making a point. Laziness, lack of clear thinking, or the desire to impress readers by the display of superior knowledge often lead writers to overlook this elementary rule. Descriptions such as :

'The Adagio, in modified ternary form, contains 'a beautiful episode for bass-trombone and flute 'unisono. Here is one of its principal motives . . .'

should be carefully eschewed if the object aimed at is criticism.

CHAPTER V

ETHICS, TACTICS, AND POINTS
FOR BEGINNERS

1

' The critic, let it not be forgotten, is in business
' for himself, not for the composer. He is not here
' to see that the name of Brown or Jones is kept before
' the public eye : that is Brown's or Jones's own affair.
' He is here to talk the soundest and most enduring
' sense possible to him about art and artists.' Thus
Ernest Newman (*Sunday Times*, 29 May 1922). Another view, more altruistic, possibly a trifle vainglorious
or quixotic, is that his first duty is to do all he can in
aid of the causes he believes in. Although there may
be no question that, in the long run, it is only by
talking ' the soundest and most enduring sense possible ' that he may hope to contribute directly to the
education of his public, there are reasons why he
should occasionally forgo the attitude of aloofness
which the above axiom implies, and act as Bennett's
' passionate few ' who keep on talking of the works
they love and buying them and keeping these works
before the public eye. By taking to his work seriously,
he will have acquired knowledge and facilities which
may be denied to others ; he will obtain access to
little-known works, to works which others overlook,
and may find that to be critically right with regard
to them is not all that he can do and wishes to do.

2

Whether his criticism, or any other form of activity
open to him in his capacity as a writer, may be useful

or not is a point which he may consider before he decides to become a writer on music ; but when he has taken the leap, he must steadfastly believe that it is, or at least act as if he did. Faith in his power and in the worthiness of his aims are indispensable.

J. D. M. Rorke, the author of that very instructive booklet, *A Musical Pilgrim's Progress*, has written (in *Music and Letters*, April 1922) an article advocating for the musical critic a policy very different from that which is suggested here, but in which he says that ' musical criticism would be greatly improved if it had a little more humility '. As a matter of tactics, let us say. that humility may prove more useful in the critic's workshop than in his shop-window. It should be present in the spirit in which results are sought, but not necessarily in the utterance. Indeed, a leader (and leadership should be the true critic's ultimate aim) may lose as much by lacking firmness as he gains by being cautious. Even when he is in doubt, he must feel confident that an attitude of doubt is the only possible one under the circumstances, and be as positive on the point as he might be when praising or blaming. Elsewhere, he may feel it incumbent upon him to make clear that his opinion is open to challenge ; but if his opinion is definite he should still express it definitely.

Let, then, the critic act as one who has a duty to perform. If he really loves music, he will feel that nothing could irk him more than to see works which he thinks great ignored or misjudged, especially while works he thinks contemptible or baneful are being extolled. And he will soon realize that to bring about redress is a difficult if not a hopeless task, a task calling for his most eager and most disinterested zeal—but one whose accomplishment may carry with it a reward more desirable, though less tangible, than the mere building up of his reputation as a critic.

He can do but little, it is true. He may write and thereby occasionally stimulate a few people to hear, study, and buy the works he praises, or (less frequently) cause some of these works to be publicly performed. He may dissuade a few people from revelling in the music whose unworthiness he exposes. Whether he succeeds or not in kindling in his readers a desire to love the works he loves and to rid themselves of their weakness for the works he holds up to reprobation, he should at least be capable of inspiring them with the wish to know the works he praises and to pay due heed to the points he brings to their notice.

A review of a recent book on Scriabin (*The Outlook*, 2 June 1923) contains a remark which the critic will do well to take to heart quite apart from its bearing upon Scriabin's music : ' The fact is that through ' indolence we have conceded the full claims of the ' Scriabinists, and have allowed to a composer who had ' fewer glimpses of the house beautiful than any of ' the Russian school a position absurdly out of place ' with his merits.'

Indolence, except perhaps with regard to their unavoidable tasks and a few hobbies, is the chief besetting sin of most critics, and a sin for which there is no excuse ; it constitutes an unfairness towards the critic's employers, towards his ̄readers, and towards the composers and performers with whom he deals.

Even the utmost a critic can do is but a drop in the ocean so far as living composers are concerned. For these, the success which should follow worthy artistic achievement is largely a matter of commercial organization and advertisement. Even public performance, the only way in which most works may reach the public, often depends upon these two factors. You may write persistently and convincingly in praise of a musical drama, a symphony, or even a quartet, and find your aims defeated by the mere fact that the work is published abroad, or that the readers whom your utterances may have interested cannot easily find out where it is procurable.

Music cannot be disseminated in the same way as books. The question is partly one of comparatively higher cost, partly one of the need for the intervention of performers (it may be as well to mention here that I am quite aware that there are such things as talking-machines, and that I do not deny the value of the aid afforded by the piano-player). Nor does there exist—except in the case of a few famous performers, some of whom, by the music they sing and play and conduct, do incalculable harm—the artificial stimulus of price inflation which plays so great a part in the fate of paintings and sometimes of painters. In short, conditions for most composers, and most certainly for the overwhelming majority of earnest composers, especially those who do not care to advertise themselves even by legitimate means, are altogether deplorable.

All this, of course, is not primarily the critic's concern. But the point, as one of ethics, is worth considering, in order to decide whether, when the critic does something—be it ever so little—to smooth the way for a composer of merit, he may not be serving his art and vindicating his own claims in the best possible way.

4

The critic's duties lie on one hand with the composers and performers, on the other with his readers. The readers, who very rightly are out for a maximum of musical enjoyment and expect from the critic advice how to achieve it within the limits of their available time, means, and experience, are entitled to be directed towards the best and the best only. The composers and performers have a right to fair play. ' The business of criticism ', Ernest Newman writes (*Sunday Times*, 27 May 1923), ' is, in the case of the first-rate

143

' artist, to see him steadily and see him whole, and in
' the case of the second- or third-rate artist, to see him
' steadily and see him damned.' It stands to reason
that it also is the business of criticism not to overlook
the possible merits of second-rate stuff, nor to grudge
comparative praise where comparative praise is due.

Even when dealing with composers whom one thinks
first rate, it is most difficult to maintain a steady
balance and apportion praise and restrictions. For
certain writers, the tendency indiscriminately to praise
all that comes from the pen of Bach, Beethoven,
Brahms, or Wagner—or of the idol of the moment—
is irresistible.

One of the critic's greatest difficulties is to make
clear the differences between works that are merely
good and works that really matter, as between works
that are merely indifferent and works that are bad
enough to exercise a nefarious influence.

The following remarkable defence of second-rate
music contains views which I certainly do not endorse,
but which in principle are not unworthy of consideration. 'Works of comparatively inferior merit, if
' sincere and artistic and musicianly, act as a lever to
' raise the taste of the musical public. They are, as
' it were, a " half-way house " between what is abso-
' lutely worthless and what seems to be inspired from
' heaven. . . . There are different strata of the emo-
' tions. . . . Music, therefore, that represents a some-
' what lower standard of expression has a place and
' a purpose in artistic life.' (Claude W. Parnell,
Musical Opinion, February 1923, p. 447.)

It is difficult to see how a work may be of comparatively inferior merit if it is ' artistic and musicianly ', but we may admit that inferior works may
be artistic and musicianly *to a degree*. And the student,
in the course of his analyses of his vocabulary, will do
well to investigate the difference between sincerity
(a matter of purpose) and genuineness (a matter of

achievement). The worst composers may be as sincere as the greatest ; but their utterances are not equally genuine. However, the point of principle made by the writer was worth making, if only as a warning against overstatement.

5

As regards overstatement, the student had better set his mind at rest forthwith : however hard a critic tries to avoid it, he will overstate now and then, and is doomed to overstate. By nature the critic is a man of strong likes, dislikes, and beliefs ; and as such, even if he never allows himself to be carried away by the desire to make his point, he will usually express himself whole-heartedly, and therefore not always steer clear of exaggeration. Most readers know better than to take all the critic's utterances without a pinch of salt. But for his own guidance, the student should learn to discriminate between overstatement that merely exaggerates and overstatement that amounts to distortion.

6

The critic is often judged by his loves rather than by his methods. The public who look to him for guidance (and not infrequently for guidance of the kind provided by guides to galleries and other ' places of public interest ') want facts, like Thomas Gradgrind, and take their stand accordingly. But the point of view of those who are in quest of education is equally worthy of consideration. It is the critic whose methods are soundest who will eventually prove the best educator.

The test of his soundness will be found in his way of dealing with new music and unknown music. Nothing is simpler in a general way than to be sound on the classics. A very little experience in the art of writing and a moderately well-stocked reference library are all that is wanted. Nothing is safer and easier

145

than to repeat, with or without variations, the ortho-
dox views on Bach, Beethoven, Mozart, Schumann,
Handel, and others. A dozen essays or a quarter-
dozen books on these lines will suffice to build up
a reputation for soundness—as many writers have discovered who would never dream of contributing to
the solution of to-day's problems, or of older problems
yet unsolved, or even of adding to the available stock
of knowledge on the very topics they deal with.

Even when a critic offers an original and valuable
contribution on an acknowledged classic, he is pre-
vented from going astray by the simple fact that the
spade-work has been done before, blind alleys have
been closed, and the right road mapped out in its
essentials, or at least opened. But he who writes
to-day on Bartòk or Schönberg or Kodály or Koechlin
lacks specific aid where such aid is most needed. He
has to do all the spade-work which each particular
case calls for in proportion as it is out of the common.
He cannot hope to deal with his topic as thoroughly
as he might when he has more data and greater
facilities for seeing things in their true perspective ;
but if his methods are sound, whatever he will do will
hold good so far as it goes.

7

Another of the critic's misfortunes is that he will
often find it difficult to avoid, and even to detect, the
form of unfairness which consists in not holding the
balance even between composers whose tendencies and
achievements happen to provide a peg on which to
hang his disquisitions and the others. It is easy enough
to fail in this respect, because it is far the simplest,
even when dealing with music, to write about anything but music—that is, music from the point of
view of its intrinsic beauty and significance. It is
even easier to appear to fail when one is aware of the
danger ; for you can write so much more about every-

thing except the only thing that matters. Pegs of this kind are countless. With regard to Beethoven, it will be the tragedy of his life, his written dreams and self-confessions ; to Wagner, the characters and symbols in his dramas, Mathilde Wesendonck, the rights and wrongs of the leitmotives ; to Liszt, Strauss, Scriabin, the poetic, dramatic, and symbolic intents and functions of their music ; to Franck, the cyclic principle ; to the Russians, nationalism, or nationality, and the use of folk-tunes. Elsewhere it will be classicism, romanticism, impressionism, expressionism, and other isms ; horizontal writing, special scales, modal harmony, atonality, polytonality. One composer rivets fetters, another smashes them.

All this may serve a purpose, at least occasionally. But in proportion as it leads to excessive digression, the attention given by both critic and public to composers whose work has to be considered apart from such adventitious aid may correspondingly decrease.

8

This final chapter is the only one in which reference is made to the task of criticizing performers of music—a task towards whose accomplishment the student may have hoped for more help than it appears possible to afford him.

For the tiro's guidance let it be remarked that criticism of interpretations bears upon two points : on one hand the interpreter's technical efficiency, on the other, his conception of the work's style, trend, and character. The former is always more nearly a matter of pure facts, the latter may be more nearly a matter of opinion, upon which the expert judges at times in accordance with his own views of the work played—when his judgement in turn should be interpreted in the light of his judgement on these works. Two critics wrote of one performance : the first, that

'the very intelligent playing of —— redeemed the
'concert for us, or would have done had the music
'been worth the fineness of style expended on it';
and the second, that 'the playing did not correspond
'in the least with the composer's intentions, the music
'being merely skimmed, so to speak, and the pregnancy
'of rhythms and colours reduced to a bare minimum'.

It is easy from this to see how their estimates of the
music played may have influenced their verdict on
the playing.

Let the beginner, then, watch himself in this matter
as in all others, remembering that when appraising
music, or the performance of music, or other people's
views on music, it is with ideas and facts that he has
to deal, not with persons. He should steadfastly avoid
giving offence, and realize that irritating people, as
a rule, will not help him towards making his point.
Sarcasm is a useful weapon at times, but flippancy, like
violence, generally defeats its own ends. The facile
smartness of the remark on Beethoven's three hundred
tonics, quoted on p. 131, aims at the same purpose
as Rimsky-Korsakof's sober utterances. Whether it
will achieve its end equally well is an open question.
A true sense of humour—that gift so rarely conferred
upon musical critics—will help to decide such points
and many others. It will tell you whether you score
as surely as your sense of proportion will tell you
whether the point is worth scoring.

In any case, remember that you are out to help, not
merely to win marks, or domineer, or strike triumphant
attitudes. So long as you abide by this principle you
will have little difficulty in doing the best that it lies
in your power to do.